The Yearbook digital edition

From now on you will be able to study the Yearbook on your iPad or iPhone or on your Android device. We will add an app for Windows PC soon.

The digital edition allows you to replay all the moves on the interactive chessviewer, so you will no longer need a board and set to refresh your opening repertoire. Your preparation at tournaments will be better and easier since you can bring all your Yearbooks without breaking your back.

For existing Yearbook subscribers:
You will get free access to all back issues of 2016 and 2017 and all new digital issues of your current subscription. Please contact us by email if you need help activating the digital subscription: nic@newinchess.com.

For new Yearbook subscribers:
If you subscribe now, we will immediately send you the paperback Anniversary Issue. And you will get access to all digital Yearbook issues of 2016, 2017 and 2018. That is more than 300 Opening Surveys and more than 900 opening exercises.

Praise from a beta-tester:
'The application is amazing. Please bring out older Yearbooks as well. I use them a lot'
Daniel Montoya, San Francisco

Now available for iPad, iPhone and Android
Please have a look at the free apps: www.newinchess.com/chess-apps
Soon available on Windows PC

Opening ideas – Novelties – Book Reviews – Theory – Discussions – Gambits

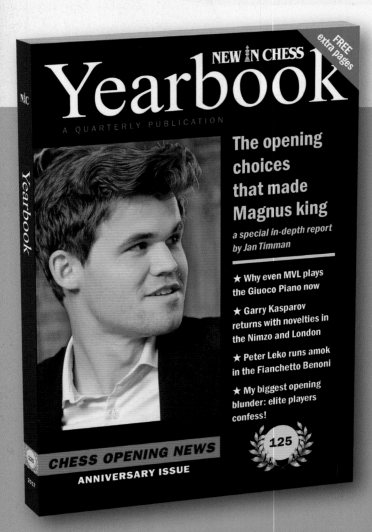

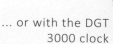

2017#8

NEW IN CHESS

Contents

'Paul Morphy was sooo far ahead of his peers.'

CONTRIBUTORS TO THIS ISSUE
Erwin l'Ami, Jeroen Bosch, Maxim Dlugy, Anish Giri, John Henderson, Alexandra Kosteniuk, Ding Liren, Dylan McClain, Ashot Nadanian, Peter Heine Nielsen, Maxim Notkin, Alejandro Ramirez, Hans Ree, Matthew Sadler, Nigel Short, Aryan Tari, Jan Timman, Jennifer Vallens, Mark Wieder

Warhol Chess

Andy Warhol's *Campbell's Soup Cans* is one of the most enduring icons in modern art, catching the zeitgeist of the early sixties and mass consumerism. Initially created as a series of canvases in 1962, the soup cans gained inter-

national acclaim as a break-through in Pop Art, with Warhol declared a genius, being the father of the modern meme as artistic expression.

Warhol created thirty-two canva-ses, covering all the flavours of his favourite soup. Now we all

know that thirty-two makes a chess set – and that's exactly the thinking that Kidrobot (the premier creator and dealer of limited edition art toys) must have had when they partnered recently with The Andy Warhol Foundation, with the collabora-

tion seeing the release in early November of a collectible chess set featuring the late artist's famed Campbell's soup cans. The iconic pieces in turn act as the chess figures, while the multi-coloured board comes complete with felt accents. Each

vinyl three-inch Campbell's soup can is labelled and printed on top with its corresponding piece to avoid confusion. The Andy Warhol / Kidrobot Campbell's Soup Can collector's chess set is now on sale for $500 at www.kidrobot.com ■

Iceland's beautiful passion

In early October, the national football team of Iceland – who were the revelation of the 2016 Euro Championship with their stunning run to the quarter-finals, winning over many friends in the process – sealed a place in the World Cup in Russia 2018 with a 2-0 victory against Kosovo in Reykjavik. With this feat they became the smallest country ever to qualify for the finals. Of course, footballers have many ways to unwind after the stresses of such a big match, but Emil Hallfredsson fittingly did so by indulging in his country's other passion by playing chess!

Immediately after the match, the Udinese and Iceland midfielder chose to mark the historic moment with a game of, er, naked chess, wearing nothing more than just a pair of bright red slippers, with his trusty shooting boots by his side. 'The art of chess wearing shoes,' Hallfredsson wrote on his Instagram to explain

Iceland's Emil Hallfredsson and 'the art of chess wearing shoes'.

the picture, as he looked extremely focused – not to mention extremely bereft of clothing – on the game.

I know it so well

'Nothing is so good it lasts eternally; perfect situations must go wrong' – so went the opening line to the lovelorn duet *I Know Him So Well* with Elaine Page and Barbara

Dickson, the big global smash hit of 1985 that remains in the record books as the best-selling female duet of all time. It comes, of course, from the concept musical *Chess*, written by Tim Rice and Abba's Benny Andersson and Björn Ulvaeus, yet

Benny Andersson and Tim Rice. 'He told us we were first choice!'

those prophetic words could well have been the story itself to the musical.

Set against the backdrop of the Cold War, all about a world championship contest between an American and Soviet grandmaster who fight over a woman, the musical had a triumphant premier in London's West End in 1986, only to sensationally flop two years later on Broadway after being eviscerated by New York Times critic Frank Rich.

But now *Chess* is set for a West End revival in early spring next year by the English National Opera, with Rice and Andersson – both big chess addicts – making the announcement official when they appeared on the BBC's The Andrew Marr Show in late November. It will run at the London Coliseum, and will be directed by Laurence Connor, whose recent theatre credits include *School of Rock* and *Miss Saigon* both on Broadway and in the West End.

Casting is now well underway, the tickets are scheduled to go on sale by the end of the year, and Rice claimed this would be the 'definitive' stage version and will be a bit more chess-savvy than the original. The famed lyricist also admitted that Benny and Björn were

not his first choice of partners. Originally he approached his early collaborator from *Jesus Christ Superstar* and *Evita*, Andrew Lloyd Webber, and although initially interested he was far too busy working on his own smash hit *The Phantom of the Opera*.

Rice then sounded out the acclaimed American composer Marvin Hamlisch, but he too was preoccupied with another project. It was only after this setback, he said he turned his attention to the boys from Abba – all of which came as news to Benny Andersson, who jokingly intersected that Rice had always reassured them that they were his first and only choice for *Chess*!

Closing Gambit

The Internet Movie Database has put online the official trailer for *Closing Gambit (1978 – Korchnoi vs Karpov & The Kremlin)*, a major new feature documentary of that epic chess showdown between the Russian dissident and the Soviet loyalist in

The epic 1978 Karpov-Kortchnoi showdown.

the Philippines, which will premier during next year's Cannes Film Festival in the spring.

It's written and directed by Alan Byron of A2B Media in the UK, who produces music documentaries and biographies for international distribution, such as the BBC, Sky, The Biography Channel and many others. Unlike most other documentaries and films on chess, Byron, 52, is no stranger to the game himself, as he's been a lifelong semi-serious player with a FIDE rating, who has played in international opens, as well as the European Club Cup and the 4NCL – so he at least lived through every move, every kick, and most likely every flavour of yogurt from that epic Kortchnoi-Karpov Baguio City match of 1978.

The 3-minute plus trailer shows lots of wonderful archive footage from the match and offers glimpses of interviews with numerous grandmasters, including Anatoly Karpov himself, Michael Stean and Ray Keene, Kortchnoi's seconds for the match, and Garry Kasparov. So get your popcorn at the ready, as this documentary looks one not to miss when it goes on general release in mid-2018!

Board to the boardroom

Lord Price, who spent decades at the helm of Britain's biggest companies and till recently was a government minister representing the nation's trade interests on the global stage, revealed in an interview what was the secret of his boardroom success: mastering chess at a young age.

He stepped down in early September as minister of state for trade and investment in order to pursue 'business and writing interests', and told the *Daily Telegraph* on leaving government that the skills he learned from playing chess at school have proved invaluable for him in business. 'You need to try and understand the game from your opponent's point of view,' he said.

Lord Price believes chess should be taught early to children.

'So much of life is about thinking about the people around you – what are they thinking? What are they going to do?' And this, he admitted, is where his early chess prowess came to the fore.

Lord Price firmly believes that games like chess that develop strategic thinking are really important to business people as they develop their career. He is so passionate about the importance of chess that he believes it should be taught early to children, and therefore he has written a children's book named *The Foolish King: The Secret History of Chess*, a fairy tale about how our game came about.

He got the brainwave when he taught his eldest daughter – who is now 22-years-old – how to play chess when she was six. 'I made up a story to help her understand how all the pieces move.'

In 2016, Lord Price turned that fairy tale into an app and a book for children. And now he has written a sequel to *The Foolish King* – written under his non-titled name of Mark Price – which is due to be published next year.

Do the hustle

The *New York Post* published an intriguing story about Ambakisye Osayaba, a former city cleaner for Central Park, who six years ago had the temerity to quit the day job for a life of chess, and now claims he earns $400 a day as one of the game's top street hustlers.

Whilst Washington Square Park is the more fabled chess hustling haunt, Osayaba can be found sitting at his 2-by-2-foot fold-out table, chairs and chess board in New York's Union Square Park every day, rain or shine. He charges $3 a game. If you think you can beat him, the wager is $5. He charges $20 for a 30 minute lesson. 'It's the best living I've ever made,' says Osayaba.

The 59-year-old told the *NY Post* that he's earned some big wins through chess, including $600 from a nearby Best Buy worker who was foolish enough to keep on doubling bets while

Ambakisye Osayaha: no regrets.

on a losing streak. Osayaba is also said to have befriended one of America's leading players and, more than likely, probably made a lifetime enemy of another. The late Bill Lombardy (see the obituary in this issue -ed.) used to chill with Osayaba and taught him much about the game. 'He used to hang out here with us all the time,' he said. 'In the summer he'd even sleep out here with us when we'd play all night.'

The other high-profile contact was Hikaru Nakamura, whom Osayaba met during the Karjakin-Carlsen World Championship Match in New York. 'Nakamura was acting like a jerk,' alleges our in-the-money street hustler, so instead he ended up playing an informal game with the US No.3's girlfriend, Maria De Rosa, who is one of Italy's leading women players. Osayaba beat her, with the help of Lombardy: 'He was singing the moves at me while I played her.' ∎

A World of Chess. *Its Development and Variations through Centuries and Civilizations.* Jean-Louis Cazaux *and* Rick Knowlton. 2017, $49.95 softcover (17.8 × 25.4 cm), 408pp., 71 illus., 297 diagrams, 9 maps, notes, bibliography, indexes, 978-0-7864-9427-9. Immense, deeply researched: the Persian and Arab game familiar for 500 years; similar games going back 1500 years still played; evolution of strategic board games especially in India, China and Japan; more recent chess variants (board sizes, new pieces, 3-D etc.).

W.H.K. Pollock. *A Chess Biography with 524 Games.* Olimpiu G. Urcan *and* John S. Hilbert. 2017, $65 library binding (18.4 × 26 cm), 508pp., 68 illustrations, diagrams, tables, appendices, notes, bibliography, index, 978-0-7864-5868-4. Englishman Pollock (1859–1896) played in many important American events of the 1800s and numerous matches against strong players. "Wonderful...superb"—*Chessbook Reviews;* "A perfect marriage of subject, author and publisher. Open at random and be entertained."—Jonathan Manley, editor, *Kingpin Chess Magazine;* HONORABLE MENTION, BOOK OF THE YEAR AWARD—*Chess Journalists of America.*

H.E. Bird. *A Chess Biography with 1,198 Games.* Hans Renette. 2016, $75 library binding (21.9 × 28.5 cm), 608pp., 1,198 games, 376 diagrams, 85 illustrations, tables, appendices, notes, bibliography, indexes, 978-0-7864-7578-0. No 19th century player had a longer career — nor more slashing attack games — than Henry Edward Bird (1829–1908). A detailed account of his personal life and vigorous feats. BOOK OF THE YEAR AWARD—*Chess Journalists of America.*

Vera Menchik. *A Biography of the First Women's World Chess Champion, with 350 Games.* Robert B. Tanner. 2016, $49.95 library binding (18.4 × 26 cm), 328pp., 21 photographs, appendices, bibliography, indexes, 978-0-7864-9602-0. The first woman to compete on an equal basis with the top male players. She dominated women's chess for 17 years. Games include notes by her, Capablanca, Alekhine, Fine, others. "Incredible collection of games...a must-have...quality and clarity of material makes it unique"—*Georgia Chess News.*

José Raúl Capablanca. *A Chess Biography.* Miguel A. Sánchez. 2015, $55 library binding (18.4 × 26 cm), 563pp., 195 annotated games, 55 illustrations, appendices, notes, bibliography, indexes, 978-0-7864-7004-4. "Amazing"—*Huffington Post;* "even the most ardent Capa fan will learn something new"—*Chess Life;* "a luxurious work and a true labor of love"—*Chess News;* "first rate...highly recommended"— IM John Donaldson (*JeremySilman.com*).

Boilly, Louis Leopold (1761–1845). *The Chess Game.* Josse/Scala/Art Resource, NY.

Samuel Lipschütz. *A Life in Chess.* Stephen Davies. 2015, $65 library binding (18.4 × 26 cm), 408pp., 249 games, 42 illustrations, appendices, bibliography, indexes, 978-0-7864-9596-2. "Valuable collectors' item...beautifully printed...history at its best"—*British Chess Magazine;* "a great discovery"—*Huffington Post;* "highly recommended"— IM John Donaldson (*Jeremy Silman.com*).

Joseph Henry Blackburne. *A Chess Biography.* Tim Harding. 2015, $75 library binding (21.9 × 28.5 cm), 592pp., *1,186 games,* 95 illustrations, appendices, notes, bibliography, indexes, 978-0-7864-7473-8. "Comprehensive...beautiful"—*Huffington Post;* "a great love for detail...a breathtaking and carefully researched masterpiece"—*Chess News;* "definitive...indispensable"—*Chess Life.*

Mikhail Botvinnik. *The Life and Games of a World Chess Champion.* Andrew Soltis. 2014, $49.95 library binding (18.4 × 26 cm), 282pp., 107 annotated games, 127 diagrams, photographs, notes, bibliography, indexes, 978-0-7864-7337-3. "Brilliant...the best book on Botvinnik by far"—*Chess News* "another Soltis tour-de-force...fascinating"— IM John Donaldson (*JeremySilman.com*); BOOK OF THE YEAR— English Chess Federation. BOOK OF THE YEAR AWARD—*Chess Journalists of America.*

Ignaz Kolisch. *The Life and Chess Career.* Fabrizio Zavatarelli. 2015, $75 library binding (21.9 × 28.5 cm), 360pp., 324 games, 174 diagrams, 63 illustrations, appendices, notes, bibliography, indexes, 978-0-7864-9690-7. The Hungarian (1837–1889) champion and financier. "One of the most accurate chess books that McFarland has ever published"— Edward Winter, *Chess Notes;* "remarkable"—*Huffington Post;* FINALIST, BOOK OF THE YEAR— English Chess Federation.

The Classical Era of Modern Chess. Peter J. Monté. 2014, $65 library binding (18.4 × 26 cm), 616pp., 155 illustrations, glossary, appendices, bibliography, index, 978-0-7864-6688-7. "Prodigious scholarship...the erudition, the care, and the enormous effort which went into it is obvious"— Dale Brandreth, *Caissa Editions;* "one of the most important chess books published in the last twenty years... highly recommended"— IM John Donaldson (*JeremySilman.com*); "[this] brilliant, exhaustive work is unique in chess history...an absolute must"—*Huffington Post;* HONORABLE MENTION, BOOK OF THE YEAR AWARD—*Chess Journalists of America.*

Random pairings

Concerning the opinions expressed by GMs Timman and Hammer in the Isle of Man article in New In Chess 2017/7, I have some familiarity with that pairing system. One Long Island NY organizer uses it in all of his one night per week events, frequently without announcing such a major pairing variation in his advertising (a violation of US Chess Federation rules), which has cost him several formerly regular participants.

Player 1 vs. Player 2 has occurred in Round 1 (ridiculous in a short event, leading Player 2 to often take a Round 1 bye to avoid same; of course if Player 1 has the same idea, they could end up as a forced pairing in Round 2 if there are no draws in Round 1). The regular system is much better and it also gives you the chance to prepare for the next opponent, if you're willing to put the work in, whereas random (aleatory! Thank you, Nigel!) doesn't.

The normal pairing system does not hurt the lower rated players. The fastest way to improve is by playing stronger players, not grovelling among fellow patzers. One leading US organizer gives free entry prizes to junior prize-winners, with the proviso that they use them by entering the strongest possible (Open) section. The way to improve is by running the gauntlet of stronger players and one must earn the way up that ladder of/ to success.

What happened this time, Nigel? No new four syllable word in the latest 'Diamonds are forever' article? Or were the multisyllabic names of your hosts too exhausting ☺?

Edward Frumkin
New York, NY, USA

Judit's concept of chess

In New In Chess 2017/5, Judit Polgar comments on 46.♖b7 in Leko-Nybäck: '... the most subtle point being that 46...♕xd5 loses to 47.♖b8.' This combination struck me, as I found it simply gorgeous, and I was delighted to learn something new, or

already forgotten, after more than 35 years of practice.

But waking up the next day my first thought was: how can this possibly work? What if 47...♔g7 ? And the computer immediately confirms that this move saves Black, and that instead the 'immediate threat' 47.♕c7 that Judit mentions is the only winning move.

But the magic was not broken when I understood what Judit meant. If in the position after 46...♕xd5 you move the g6-pawn back to its initial square

---

Write to us
New In Chess, P.O. Box 1093
1810 KB Alkmaar, The Netherlands
or e-mail: editors@newinchess.com
Letters may be edited or abridged

---

g7, then Judit's move suddenly also wins. And it is even more beautiful if you push the black pawn on e5 to e4, because then 47.♕c7 does not win any longer.

This says a lot, by the way, about the role of pattern recognition, and of the computer, in Judit's concept of chess.

Niels Borne
Lyon, France

Formats and time controls

As much as I enjoy your magazine, I find it frustrating to read about a competition with no mention of its format. Equally frustrating is to go over a game with no information on its time control.

Regarding the Xtracon Open, Jan Timman stated in New In Chess 2017/6: 'I was thinking a player would need 8½ points to win.' Okay, out of how many rounds? I assume, since it's an open, that the tournament is a Swiss System. Every tournament piece could easily specify '10 round SS', '12 RR', '8 double RR', or whatever the case may be, so that the report on the event is more meaningful to us readers.

And in what other competition are the spectators kept in the dark about the

time control? Sometimes the game reports mention 'rapid', 'classical', or 'blitz', but even within these parameters time controls can vary. Please put at the heading of each game '20-i10', 'G/120', '30-d5', '40/2 + SD/30i5', or whatever the time control was for that game.

In the same issue Teimour Radjabov said that he made the move 38.♖xg7 'when I was down to one second'. Was that one second until move 40? For the rest of the game? What was the delay or increment? This reader does not like to be left guessing.

Denny Helmuth
Wooster, Ohio, USA

Editorial Postscript

Thank you for this suggestion. Generally we try to make it as clear as possible what kind of time controls were used – albeit not as detailed as you suggest – and the number of rounds and the format are indicated in the tournament tables. It would be good to hear from more readers if they'd prefer more detailed descriptions of the time controls as well.

COLOPHON

PUBLISHER: Allard Hoogland
EDITOR-IN-CHIEF:
Dirk Jan ten Geuzendam
HONORARY EDITOR: Jan Timman
CONTRIBUTING EDITOR: Anish Giri
EDITORS: Peter Boel, René Olthof
ART-DIRECTION: Jan Scholtus
PRODUCTION: Joop de Groot
TRANSLATORS: Ken Neat, Piet Verhagen
SALES AND ADVERTISING: Remmelt Otten

PHOTOS AND ILLUSTRATIONS IN THIS ISSUE:
Alina l'Ami, Frank Anderson, Valeriy Belobeev,
Maria Emelianova, Lennart Ootes, Macauley Peterson,
Ole Kristian Strom, Berend Vonk
COVER PHOTO: Alina l'Ami

© No part of this magazine may be reproduced, stored in a retrieval system or transmitted in any form or by any means, recording or otherwise, without the prior permission of the publisher.

NEW IN CHESS
P.O. BOX 1093
1810 KB ALKMAAR
THE NETHERLANDS

PHONE: 00-31-(0)72-51 27 137
SUBSCRIPTIONS: nic@newinchess.com
EDITORS: editors@newinchess.com
ADVERTISING: otten@newinchess.com

WWW.NEWINCHESS.COM

Peak Rankings of the Candidates, Then and Now

The field for the 2018 Candidates tournament is set, and by any measure, it is impressive. There is one ex-world champion (Vladimir Kramnik) and the players currently ranked Nos. 2, 3, and 4 in the world (Levon Aronian, Fabiano Caruana, and Shakhriyar Mamedyarov, respectively). But how does the 2018 group stack up against the field from 2016? And what about the two players who fell short

of qualifying on the final day of the Grand Prix (Maxime Vachier-Lagrave and Teimour Radjabov)?

The graphic below looks at the peak rankings of all the players in the 2016 and 2018 Candidates, or who were in the running to be in next year's competition. Readers can judge who, if anyone, will be missed the most.

DYLAN LOEB McCLAIN

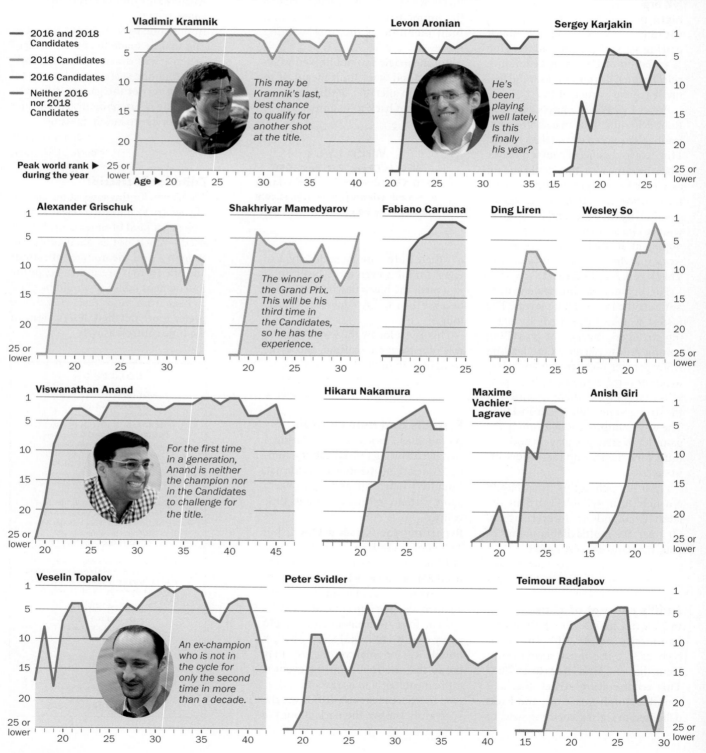

— 2016 and 2018 Candidates
— 2018 Candidates
— 2016 Candidates
— Neither 2016 nor 2018 Candidates

Peak world rank ▶ during the year

Vladimir Kramnik
This may be Kramnik's last, best chance to qualify for another shot at the title.

Levon Aronian
He's been playing well lately. Is this finally his year?

Sergey Karjakin

Alexander Grischuk

Shakhriyar Mamedyarov
The winner of the Grand Prix. This will be his third time in the Candidates, so he has the experience.

Fabiano Caruana

Ding Liren

Wesley So

Viswanathan Anand
For the first time in a generation, Anand is neither the champion nor in the Candidates to challenge for the title.

Hikaru Nakamura

Maxime Vachier-Lagrave

Anish Giri

Veselin Topalov
An ex-champion who is not in the cycle for only the second time in more than a decade.

Peter Svidler

Teimour Radjabov

Lewis Hamilton: 'It is a bit like a game of chess, right now it is at check but there is still a long way to go.'
(The Formula 1 champion's chessic description to the media about his long battle with Ferrari driver Sebastian Vettel before the U.S. Grand Prix in Austin, Texas, ahead of clinching the 2017 drivers' crown)

Roy Keane: 'I'm sure there is [research] that's ongoing. But if you're worried about the physical side of any sport, you're wary of it, then play chess.'
(The former Manchester United star and current Ireland assistant boss when asked about the possible link between dementia and heading a football)

John Healy: 'As my old cell mate Harry the Fox who taught me chess used to say about chess, "What else is it but breaking and entering when you force your way into your opponent's castled position, hi-jack his pieces, steal his pawns, capture his Queen and mug his King in broad daylight?"'
(The Grass Arena author in his review of Carl Portman's new book, Chess Behind Bars)

John Urschel: 'It's because the things I love the most in this world (reading math, doing research, playing chess) are very, very inexpensive.'
(The chess-mad NFL star who shocked the game by recently retiring early to pursue a PhD at MIT, and explaining to the US media why instead he chose to drive a used car and live on $25,000 a year)

Idris Elba: 'If I didn't want to be recognised I would've been a chess player. I'm in the wrong profession to complain about being recognised.'
(The English actor, producer, musician and DJ on the toll of fame in The Daily Express)

Jane Fonda: 'When you've been married and then divorced, and the husband has died and decades have now gone past, and you see these pictures of happiness - and yeah, he did teach me how to play chess better. So yes, we were happy.'
(The legendary screen actress in the new BBC documentary, David Hurn: A Life in Pictures, as she reunites for the first time in 50 years with the Magnum photographer who shot most of her private life with film screenwriter and director husband, Roger Vadim)

Tim Vine: 'So, I ate this chess set. It was horrible. I took it back to the shop. I said, "This is stale, mate." He said, "Are you sure?" I said, "Check, mate."'
(The English writer, actor, comedian and presenter, known for his quick-fire puns)

Anton Kovalyov: 'I know that I'm not the brightest person, but I feel that I'm not stupid enough to testify against FIDE.'
(The Ukrainian-born Canadian GM explains why he didn't testify during the hearing of his case at the recent FIDE Congress in Antalya, Turkey)

Boris Spassky: 'I love chess but I hate my profession… I am not competitive.' *(Admitted the former World Champion over a 1984 lunch conversation with Andy Soltis)*

Bobby Fischer: 'I do not believe in heroes.'
(On turning down an offer from the Mayor of New York for a ticker-tape parade along Fifth Avenue after winning the world title in 1972)

Yuzvendra Chahal: 'Chess has helped me in increasing my patience. There are times when a bowler doesn't get a wicket and he panics. This doesn't happen with me. Chess has given me this advantage in cricket. I don't get panic when I don't get wickets.'
(The former Indian youth chess star-turned-cricketer, who is now one of India's promising leg-spinners)

Lennox Lewis: 'If you teach a kid chess, you teach him to sit down and think.' *(The 3-time heavyweight champion boxer, who has funded an after-school chess program for disadvantaged youths)*

The Game of the Year

Ding Liren himself on his gem of lasting beauty

A sensational queen sacrifice crowned by a brilliant rook manoeuvre that you will not easily forget. Enjoy this masterpiece with the exclusive notes of the Master himself, China's number one and the first-ever Chinese player to qualify for the Candidates' tournament.

NOTES BY DING LIREN

Bai Jinshi
Ding Liren
China 2017
Nimzo-Indian Defence, Three Knights

This is the most beautiful game I have played so far in my career. It was played on November 4, less than two weeks after I had celebrated my 25th birthday on October 24. The occasion was the match between Hangzhou and my team of Zhejiang in the Chinese League. The Chinese League continues to attract more and more strong foreign players, but of course the majority remain Chinese. My opponent was Bai Jinshi, a talented junior, born in 1999. I know him quite well. He studies very hard and he has many ideas in the opening. It was clear to me that with White he wanted to play for a win.

I felt very excited after this game. During the next days the game and the variations kept popping up in my head all the time. Even when I was lying in bed at night positions would appear in my mind, and new tries by White that I had to refute. Every time I would try to find a solution and prove that the sacrifice was sound.

The following notes are based on my thoughts during the game and what I discovered afterwards.

1.d4 ♞f6 2.c4 e6 3.♞c3 ♝b4 4.♞f3 0-0 5.♝g5 c5 6.e3 cxd4

7.♕xd4 This continuation is not so popular in this line of the Nimzo-Indian. Normally people take back with the e-pawn, 7.exd4, and after 7...d5 Carlsen went 8.♝e2 against me in St. Louis (½-½, 36).

7...♞c6 8.♕d3 The other plan is to go 8.♕f4, but after 8...♝xc3+ 9.bxc3 h6 10.♝xf6 ♕xf6 11.♕xf6 gxf6 Black has no problems at all.

8...h6 9.♝h4 d5 10.♖d1

This came as a surprise to me. I had been expecting 10.a3, when after 10...♝xc3+ 11.♕xc3 g5 12.♝g3 ♞e4 Black is fine.

10...g5 Following my plan.

11.♝g3 ♞e4

If I had seen his next move, I might have chosen the safer 11...♞a5 12.a3 (after 12.♝e2? ♞e4 White loses a pawn) 12...♝xc3+ 13.♕xc3 ♕xc3+ 14.bxc3 ♞e4, with an approximately equal position.

12.♞d2 This is a good move, which I had not expected. Now things are not so easy.

12...♞c5 This interesting continuation appealed to me.

I didn't want to play the position after 12...♝xc3 13.bxc3 ♞xg3 14.hxg3 ♚g7, when I am very passive.

And 12...f5 would be a mistake, as after 13.cxd5 exd5 14.♞dxe4 I cannot take with the d-pawn, 14...dxe4?, in view of 15.♕c4+.

13.♕c2

This he played very quickly, showing that he was still in his preparation. I had expected 13.♕b1, when I intended 13...d4 14.exd4 ♕xd4, also with a very complicated position that needs to be analysed.

13...d4 14.♞f3 e5

Fortunately I have this move, as otherwise I would just lose a pawn. Now he thought deeply for about 25 or 30 minutes, but I had also spent quite some time already.

15.♞xe5 The other way to take was with the bishop: 15.♝xe5 ♞xe5 16.♞xe5. During the game I was worried about this position, till I found 16...♖e8, which is very strong.

ANALYSIS DIAGRAM

And now there are two lines:

A) 17.♞f3 leads to a really long and

forced line, but it is also very beautiful: 17...♝f5 18.♕xf5 dxc3 19.♖xd8 c2+ 20.♚e2 c1♕ 21.♞e5

ANALYSIS DIAGRAM

This looks very dangerous, threatening mate in 2, but... 21...♕xb2+ 22.♚f3 ♕xe5 23.♕xe5 ♖axd8 24.♕b2 a5 (very important) 25.a3 ♖d2 (still all forced) 26.♕a1 ♞e4 27.axb4 ♖xf2+ 28.♚g4 ♞f6+ 29.♚g3 ♞e4+ 30.♚h3 ♖d2 31.g3 ♞f2+ 32.♚g2 ♖xe3 33.♕xa5 ♞d3+ 34.♚h3 (stepping out of the perpetual with 34.♚g1 loses to 34...♞e5) 34...♞f2+, with a draw.

B) 17.exd4 ♞e6 (this move and the capture on d4 next are not easy to find) 18.♕e4 ♞xd4 19.♕xd4 (clearly better than 19.♖xd4? ♕f6 20.♖d5 ♝e6 21.♖b5 ♝d7, and White is in deep trouble) 19...♕a5, with equality.

15...dxc3

Taking the knight and sacrificing my queen. When I decided to sac the queen, I didn't see everything, of course, but I did see 18...♞a4, and I realized that Black should be better.

16.♖xd8

In case of 16.♞xc6 Black has the strong 16...♝f5, which we both saw and which wins immediately for Black.

16...cxb2+

17.♔e2?

This is a serious mistake, after which he had lost all chances to save the game.

The other option was 17.♖d2, which turns out to be a better move, but with accurate play Black can still equalize: 17...♖d8 18.♘f3 (18.♗d3 looks attractive, but we both missed 18...♘xe5, when after 19.♗h7+ ♔f8 20.♗xe5 ♖xd2 21.♕xd2 ♗xd2+ 22.♔xd2 ♗e6 23.♗xb2 ♗xc4 the simplification leads to an equal position) 18...♗g4

ANALYSIS DIAGRAM

19.♕xb2 (the only move – 19.a3 is bad in view of 19...♗xf3 20.axb4 ♖xd2 21.♔xd2 ♖d8+ 22.♔c3 ♘a4+! 23.♔b3 ♗d1!) 19...♗xf3 (my intention was to play 19...♘e4, but I had missed 20.♕xb4 ♘xb4 21.♖b2, and now it is White who is slightly better) 20.gxf3 ♖xd2 21.♕xd2 ♗xd2+ 22.♔xd2 ♖d8+, and here Black has enough compensation, for instance: 23.♔c1 (or 23.♔e2 ♖d3) 23...♘b4 24.a3 ♘bd3+ 25.♔b1

ANALYSIS DIAGRAM

25...f5! (none of these moves are easy to find) 26.♗e2 f4 27.exf4 gxf4 28.♗h4 ♖e8 29.♗xd3 ♘xd3 30.♖d1 ♖e1, and this position is equal.

17...♖xd8 18.♕xb2 ♘a4!!

I think he had missed this move. After 18...♖d2+ 19.♕xd2 ♗xd2

20.♘xc6 White would be slightly better.

19.♕c2 There is no choice.

19...♘c3+ 20.♔f3 ♖d4!!

The key move, and a very beautiful one. I had seen it after he played 18.♕xb2 and I double-checked 18...♘a4. I got very excited when I saw I could play this move, and after I had made it many other players started thronging around our board. I could have played 20...h5 first, and gone 21...♖d4 after 21.h3, but I could not contain myself. And it comes down to the same thing.

21.h3 h5 Threatening mate, starting with 22...g4+.

22.♗h2

History in the making. Ding Liren and Bai Jingshi have started the game that would get chess fans all around the world in raptures.

22...g4+ By now I knew that my position was winning, but also that I should be very careful.

23.♔g3 He wants to take the pawn on h5, hoping to survive.

Exchanging pawns doesn't change that much: 23.hxg4 hxg4+ 24.♔g3 ♖d2 25.♕b3 ♘e4+ 26.♔h4 ♗e7+ 27.♔h5 ♖xf2, threatening ...♖f5+.

23...♖d2 Another key move that Black needs in order to win. I had seen it when I went 20...♖d4.

24.♕b3 The queen has no good place to go to. **24...♘e4+ 25.♔h4 ♗e7+ 26.♔xh5 ♔g7**

Clearing the way for the rook to come to the h-file.

27.♗f4 The only move to prevent my plan. 27.♘xc6 ♗f5 28.♘b8 would

fail to 28...♖d8, and now the other rook joins the mating attack.

27...♗f5 I could also have gone 27...♖xf2 first; there's not much difference.

28.♗h6+ ♔h7

29.♕xb7 After 29.♘xc6 ♗g6+ 30.♔xg4 f5+ the white king is mated: 31.♔f4 ♗d6+ 32.♔f3 ♖xf2 mate.

29...♖xf2

And now I threaten 30...♘g3 mate.

30.♗g5 ♖h8 With every move I bring my pieces closer to his king, all the while threatening mate.

31.♘xf7 As 31.♕xc6 ♗g8+ 32.♗h6 ♘g3 is mate. **31...♗g6+ 32.♔xg4** 32.♔h4 would have led to a beautiful mate: 32...♗g8+ 33.♘xh8 ♗g5+ 34.♔xg4 ♘e5 mate. **32...♘e5+**

A pleased Ding Liren at his computer that shows the cruncher 20...♖d4!!

And White resigned in view of 33.♘xe5 ♗f5+ 34.♔h5 ♗g8+ 35.♗h6 ♘g3 mate, or 33.♔h4 ♗g8+ 34.♘xh8 ♗xg5 mate.

'Even when I was lying in bed at night positions would appear in my mind, and new tries by White that I had to refute.'

To be honest I did not mind that my opponent did not allow me to execute the mate on the board (see Nigel Short's opinion on this in his column – ed.). If you play a game, you do not want to be mated. I think it was a very reasonable decision of him to resign when he did.

The game looks very beautiful, but I am mostly proud of the moves 18...♘a4 and 20...♖d4. After this I knew I was winning, as long as I was careful. I am happy that my play was straightforward and that I didn't spoil it.

Even though this was my most beautiful game, I continue to see Kasparov's win against Topalov in Wijk aan Zee in 1999 as the most beautiful game ever. He had to take crucial decisions on practically every turn after his sacrifice. For me this was only these two moves. ∎

For a contest in which the last two spots in the highly anticipated Candidates tournament – coming March in Berlin – were to be decided, the last Grand Prix in Mallorca was a remarkably low-key event. Billed as the Palma de Mallorca GP, the games were actually played in Playa de Mallorca, a stretch of beach and holiday hotels some 10 kilometres from the capital. The venue was the Iberostar Bahia de Palma Hotel, a four-star hotel closed for the season, where the tournament took place in a temporarily reopened area on the first floor. If you happened to walk past the hotel, you would have no inkling that anything was happening there, because there wasn't the slightest indication that the Grand Prix was taking place. It was only if you knew the correct door to enter that you'd be welcomed by the black and white house style of World Chess, which had turned the rooms into a relatively small but comfortable playing venue. There was even a small welcome desk with a handful of chess pins (for sale for €10 each) and complimentary bottles of Isklar, the Norwegian mineral water that also sponsors Magnus Carlsen.

The participants were staying in a hotel of the same chain across the street. This hotel was very much open and mainly filled with German tourists, primarily old-age pensioners,

DIRK JAN TEN GEUZENDAM

Mind Games in Mallorca

Mamedyarov and Grischuk watch from home as they qualify for Candidates

The end of the fourth and last leg of the FIDE Grand Prix felt a bit surreal. While Teimour Radjabov and Maxime Vachier-Lagrave saw their hopes of earning a place in the Candidates tournament go up in smoke, two GMs not present in Mallorca – Shakhriyar Mamedyarov and Alexander Grischuk – could celebrate their qualification at home. The final GP was won by Dmitry Jakovenko and Levon Aronian, who each earned 17,500 euros.

LENNART OOTES

Chief arbiter Jesus Mena and Hikaru Nakamura see that the drama is complete. Maxime Vachier-Lagrave will not play in the Candidates. The Frenchman is not winning but even losing his last-round game against Dmitry Jakovenko.

who like to spend their winters here. The hotel was so full, in fact, that the organizers had trouble finding rooms for the players' seconds, so that some of them had to move to another hotel for the final rounds.

Foreign visitor

The venue was a much quieter place. Public interest was low and the eight chairs that had been put in front of the monitors on which the games could be followed were often enough to accommodate all visitors. There were days when bigger groups came to watch, but these were exceptions. Among the handful of aficionados closely following the game was one foreign visitor. Paul Usselman from Calgary, Canada, had read about the GP and had included Mallorca in a

holiday trip to Europe. In his hotel, he had enquired how he could get tickets, but to his pleasant surprise there was no entrance fee. He fully enjoyed 'some of the best players in the world playing fighting chess'. His only regret, if there was one, was that his favourite player, Boris Gelfand, was not doing too well. In 2012, he had rooted for Gelfand in his World Championship match against Anand, for the same reason as he had rooted for George Foreman in his epic fight against Muhammad Ali: 'He had a strategy that could have worked.'

Of course, most fans were watching the games online, but it was unclear how many of them had paid 10 dollars for the official broadcast. Certainly not the 'hundreds of thousands' that World Chess talked about when they launched the 2017 Grand Prix. There remained

technical issues and the programme offered was far from a dream, with commentator Evgeny Miroshnichenko working alone from a studio in Moscow. The viewers' readiness to pay for the broadcast did not increase after they found out that World Chess had decided to show it for free on Facebook 'by way of promotion'.

Slow pace

But all this was not terribly important to the players. They had come to Mallorca to fight for the last two remaining spots in the Candidates or, in most cases, for a fair share of the €130,000 prize-fund. The number of players still in contention for the Candidates had dwindled to two after Ding Liren had earned his ticket to Berlin by reaching the final of the

Tbilisi World Cup. Only Maxime Vachier-Lagrave and Teimour Radjabov could still threaten the leaders in the overall standings, Mamedyarov and Grischuk.

As in the earlier GPs, the pace was slow. Vachier-Lagrave, in many eyes the favourite player to qualify in Mallorca, started with a win against Gelfand and then drew his next seven games. Perhaps the key game of the tournament was MVL's draw against Aronian in Round 3. If he had won that game, the Frenchman would have come very close to qualifying.

Maxime Vachier-Lagrave
Levon Aronian
Palma de Mallorca 2017 (3)

position after 35...d4

36.♖c5? White has a very pleasant position, and now, with 36.♔f1, he could have subtly reinforced his position. There is not much Black can do to free himself.
36...♗e7! 37.♖c4 ♗xb4 38.♖xb4 ♖d7

39.♔g2? But this definitely puts paid to White's winning prospects. Again, 39.♔f1 would have left Black

in a difficult situation, planning to meet 39...d3 with 40.♔e1, when, after 40...♖f8 41.♖a1 d2+ 42.♔e2, things look bleak for Black. **39...d3** Now this leads to a draw. **40.♖a1 d2 41.♖d1 ♖d4 42.♖xd4 exd4 43.♖xd2 ♖xa4 44.♖c2 ♖a5 45.♖xc7 ♖xb5 46.♖c8+ ♔f7** Draw.

Having limited the damage against one of his main rivals for first place, Aronian took the lead the next day by beating Anish Giri. The Dutchman was also on plus-1 after a win against Richard Rapport, but his encounter with Aronian was another frustrating experience against an opponent he has never beaten yet. The Armenian played in great style, making such an impression on his opponent that Giri failed to notice a slip-up that could have cost Aronian the full point.

The notes to this spectacular attacking game are by Aronian's friend and assistant Ashot Nadanian.

NOTES BY
Ashot Nadanian

Levon Aronian
Anish Giri
Mallorca 2017 (4)
English Opening

1.♘f3 ♘f6 2.c4 g6 3.♘c3 d5 4.cxd5 ♘xd5
This hybrid of the English Opening and the Grünfeld Defence is very popular at all levels these days.
5.d3 ♗g7 6.♗d2 0-0 7.g3 c5 8.h4!?

Those who closely follow Levon Aronian's games will probably have noticed that he has often pushed his pawn to h4 in the opening of late. This, in modern terms, is a new trend. When I still actively played in tournaments, I also often used similar ideas, so they are clear to me and close in spirit. White is anxious to open the h-file as quickly as possible to make it easier to reach the black king. The downside of this early march forward may be the fact that White's king remains in the centre and may also become a target. But there is an important difference with the Grünfeld Defence, in which White's central pawn is on d4. With the pawn on d3 it's harder for Black to organize a contact of pawn units in the centre, which means that the white king can feel safe for a longer time.
Levon's 8.h4!? is a new move in this position, in which 8.♗g2 has been played before.
8...♘c6
More reliable was the symmetrical answer 8...h5, especially if White's 8.h4 was a surprise for Black.
9.h5 ♘xc3 10.bxc3 c4 11.hxg6 hxg6 12.♕a4! 12.dxc4 looks very anti-positional, when after 12...♕a5 Black has easy play.
And the move 12.d4 Black would meet with a blow in centre: 12...e5!.

12...♘a5?
A bad move that leaves Black in a difficult situation. Giri was probably afraid of the line 12...cxd3 13.♕h4 f6 14.♗h6 ♕a5, which looks dangerous for both sides.
According to Levon, Black should have responded with 12...♕d5. But

Javier Ochoa, president of the Spanish Chess Federation, makes Levon Aronian's first move. The Armenian won a fine game, as Anish Giri once again found it hard to deal with his play.

20...g5?! More tenacious was 20...♘b7 21.fxg6 ♗g4.

21.♕d1!

This decisive move was made very quickly. Experienced chess players do not calculate much in such positions but rely on their intuition, because it is obvious that the attack is irresistible.

21...gxh4 22.♖xh4 ♖d8 23.♕h5

23.♕g4 was also a good move.

23...♔f8

24.♖g4?

Thinking that he could win as he wishes, Levon relaxed and made a mistake.

After the correct 24.♕g4 Black is helpless, since there is no defence against 25.♖h7.

24...♗f6?

A courtesy response. After the correct 24...♕d6 25.♖xg7 ♔xg7 26.♕g5+ ♔f8 27.♔f2 ♔e8 28.♕g7 White would have to start all over again to win.

25.♗h6+ ♔e8 26.♖g8+ ♔d7 27.d6!

Material losses cannot be avoided and so Black resigned.

∎ ∎ ∎

---

after 13.e4 ♕a5 14.♕xa5 ♘xa5 15.d4 White has a very pleasant position.

13.d4! Now, when Black does not have the move 13...e5, White will occupy the centre, block the g7-bishop, and cut off the black knight till the end of the game.

13...b6 14.♗g2 ♗b7 15.♕c2!

I like this move very much. It may seem that White allows Black to 'free' his knight, but this is an illusion.

15...♕d5 In case of 15...♘c6 White uses the fact that the bishop at b7 is blocked and wins with the sudden 16.♕e4!, transferring the queen to h4.

16.♘h4 16.♖h4, with the idea of 17.e4, also deserves attention.

16...♕d7 17.e4

This game is a good example of modern manoeuvring in the opening. By inconspicuous moves

(5.d3, 6.♗d2, 7.g3) White has avoided direct pawn contact in the centre, and started attacking from the flank (8.h4). As soon as Black threw his forces ahead to create pawn contacts in the centre (7...c5, 10...c4) White, as if in a boxing match, managed to dodge the blows and then took a dominant position in the centre when the enemy forces flew by (the c4-pawn) and no longer represented any danger.

17...e5 18.d5 There will be no opening of the centre!

18...♗c8 19.f4! ♕e7?!

Black is in complete confusion. It was necessary to use this opportunity to open some files and try to create counterplay with 19...exf4 20.gxf4 ♘b7.

20.f5! Now White gets the final attack for free.

This painful loss undermined Giri's self-confidence, and in the remainder of the tournament he was only a pale shadow of his own true self. Aronian seemed poised to win yet another big one with superior ease until a nasty cold put a spanner in the works. Following two brief draws against Ding Liren and Peter Svidler, he failed to grind down Rapport in a highly promising position and had to settle for a draw after 72 moves. The following day, against Evgeny Tomashevsky, he no longer tried to hide that he was feeling miserable and used the white pieces to make a draw in 17 moves. Aronian finished in shared first place, but it was clear to everyone that he would probably have won outright if he had been feeling better.

Radjabov's comeback

As Aronian entered the last round with a plus-2 score, no fewer than nine players were on plus-1. One of them was Teimour Radjabov, who was having an adventurous tournament full of ups and downs. In Round 2, he beat Paco Vallejo, but then lost to Hikaru Nakamura and Tomashevsky in Rounds 4 and 6. But the winner of the Geneva GP didn't knuckle under. The next day he beat Li Chao and then he won a great game against Gelfand.

NOTES BY
Anish Giri

Boris Gelfand
Teimour Radjabov
Mallorca 2017 (8)
Queen's Indian

1.d4 ♘f6 2.c4 e6 3.♘f3 b6
Teimour Radjabov generally plays the King's Indian, especially when looking for a sharp fight. In this game, however, he shows that the Queen's Indian can also be used to get a closed and complex King's Indian-

like structure. Gender neutrality at work. A Royal Indian Defence.
4.g3 ♗b7 5.♗g2 ♗e7 6.0-0 0-0 7.♘c3 ♘e4 8.♕d2

8...♘xd2!?
This old method of chopping off this bishop has become fashionable again, after modern players discovered that the engine actually considers such positions as pretty much equal.
9.♕xd2 d6 White has an abundance of plans at his disposal. The one that Boris Gelfand chooses seems a little vague to me. Placing rooks on the e- and d-files is the most natural thing in the world, but once we have reached a Czech Benoni structure after 13...e5, it quickly becomes clear that the rooks don't belong there.

10.♖ad1
Let's look at two alternatives.
After 10.d5 e5 11.e4 ♘d7 12.b4 g6 13.♗h3 a5 14.a3 ♘f6 15.♕e2 ♘e8 16.♘d2 ♗g7 17.bxa5 ♖xa5 18.a4 f5 19.♘b3 ♖a6 20.a5 White had got some play of his own, too, but Black held quite easily (½-½, 48) in Radjabov-Jobava, Tbilisi 2015.
And 10.b4 ♘d7 11.♖fd1 was the set-up chosen by Robert Markus

recently, who beat Beliavsky with it. Black should definitely improve on that game, because after 11...a5 12.b5 ♗f6 13.♖ac1 ♕e7 14.e3 g6 15.♘e1 ♗xg2 16.♔xg2 ♗g7 17.♘d3 f5 18.♕e2 ♖ad8 19.♕f3 e5 20.♕b7 ♘f6 21.dxe5 dxe5 22.c5 he had his queenside destroyed.
10...♘d7 11.♖fe1 c5! I think Boris simply forgot about this. White usually plays d5 and Black meets it with ...e5, after which it is easier for White to generate play on either side.
12.e4 I don't see how a Hedgehog without the dark-squared bishop can be good for White.
12...a6

13.d5 A clever way to try and bail out was 13.e5!?, but Boris is always ready to pick up a challenge.
13...e5

14.b3
Here 14.a4 would win a quarter of a tempo, since Black will probably end up putting his rook on b8 anyway.
14.a4 g6 15.h4 ♗c8 16.♗h3 is how I would expect such a position to be played. That said, with White not having his usual plan of grabbing space on the queenside, I don't think

he has reasons to be excited. The rooks are not well placed either and Black will try to prepare ...f7-f5 in the long term: 16...♘f6 17.♗xc8 ♕xc8, followed by ...♘h5-g7. White might pretend to want to push b4, and if Black buys it and goes ...a5, he will have a hole on b5, for what it's worth.

14...g6 15.♖f1

A sensible and, in fact, pretty typical retreat. White prepares ♘e1-♘d3 and f4, a decent plan to create some tension in the centre.

15...♗c8 16.♘e1

16...♖b8 Black would have excellent compensation for the pawn after 16...b5!? 17.cxb5 axb5 18.♘xb5 ♗a6. In fact, he will win back the pawn immediately, but then, if White consolidates on the light squares, the position will become pretty dry: 19.a4 ♗xb5 20.axb5 ♕b6 21.♘f3 ♕xb5 22.♕c2 ♖a3 23.♖b1 ♖b8 24.♘d2.

17.a4 f5

18.f4!?

The dark-squared bishop is badly missed, but at least White is about to get fully mobilized and is likely to get a lot of trades in the centre, and with it some relief and play.

18...exf4

18...♗f6 is a solid option with a fine position, too, but Teimour forces matters and gets a ...b5 break in.

19.gxf4 fxe4 20.♘xe4 b5 21.a5

Extremely risky, but quite doable. The alternative was 21.axb5 axb5 22.♘f3, with the idea of getting some easy counterplay with ♘fg5.

21...bxc4 22.bxc4 ♖b4 23.♖c1 ♘f6 24.♘g5!

24...♕xa5 Obviously risky, but Radjabov was in for it.

24...♘h5 was another option and so was 24...♗f5!?, the most solid option and the one that appeals the most to me. The idea is to meet 25.♘e6 with 25...♗xe6 26.dxe6 d5!.

25.♘d3 ♖a4 26.♕e3 ♕d8 27.♖ce1

White is fully mobilized and Black probably already regretted his pawn grabbing. Radjabov finds a way to keep things together.

27...♗f5! 28.♗h3

Black would be lost if not for the sequence that happens in the game. According to the higher powers, 28.♘e6 ♕c8 29.♘xf8 ♗xf8 30.♘e5 dxe5 31.fxe5 ♘g4 is balanced. I like

the white central pawns, but Black does have good piece play.
28...♘xd5! 29.cxd5 ♗xg5

With an excellent win in the penultimate round (playing the Royal Indian Defence!), Teimour Radjabov came very close to qualifying to the Candidates. The fairy-tale ended when he failed to complete a hat-trick on the final day.

30.♗xf5 30.fxg5 was the alternative, when after 30...♖e4 31.♕g3 ♖xe1 32.♘xe1 ♗xh3 33.♖xf8+ ♔xf8 34.♕xh3 ♕xg5+ the position is equal and somewhat similar to the game. Black has a lot of pawns for the knight and isn't risking much, but he can hardly cause any real problems here, whereas White will find it easy to generate multiple checking ideas.
30...♖xf5 31.♕e6+ ♔g7 32.fxg5 ♕xg5+ 33.♔h1 ♖a2

34.♕e7+ The endgame is drawn, but White is the player who has to come up with some kind of idea, because Black will simply start pushing his a-pawn. The alternative was definitely more practical:
34.♕e4! leads to a straightforward draw: 34...♕d2 (or 34...♕h5 35.♕e7+ ♔h6 36.♕e3+ ♔g7 37.♕e7+) 35.♕e7+ ♔h6!? (Black tries to escape the perpetual) 36.♕h4+ ♖h5 37.♕f2 ♕xf2 38.♘xf2, and this version of the endgame is a lot easier for White to play, with the knight coming into the game with full force via g4.

34...♕xe7 35.♖xe7+ ♔f8 36.♖ee1 ♖xf1+ 37.♖xf1+ ♔e7

Here White has to find a way to arrange the rook + knight tandem and get some clear play.
38.♖e1+ 38.♘f2! was the way. The knight is going to have a good career: 38...a5 39.♖e1+ ♔d7 40.♘e4, and this should be a draw.
38...♔d7

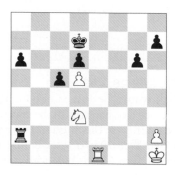

39.♖e3?! Boris finds a plan, but his pieces are not going to be in time to come back and stop both the a-pawn and the c-pawn.
39.♘f4! is the beginning of a brilliant manoeuvre suggested by the computer: 39...a5 40.♘g2!! (the best career for the knight: the c4-square) 40...a4 41.♘e3 a3 42.♘c4, and the knight beautifully controls the entire queenside.
39...a5 40.♖h3? Still part of the wrong idea. **40...h5**

41.♘f4? It is not cool to give question marks to each move, but when the plan is losing, all moves that are part of it are wrong. It is extremely hard to defend here, and it is probably already too late, but for what it's worth, the time-control was reached at this point.

41.♔g1, followed by ♘e1 and ♔f1, would have been the best defensive try, but with precise play Black should be able to win: 41...♔c7! 42.♘e1 ♖d2!.
41...a4 42.♘xg6 a3

43.♖f3 After 43.♘f4, 43...♖f2 wins on the spot. 43.♘f8+ also loses: 43...♔c7 44.♖b3 c4 45.♘e6+ ♔c8 46.♖c3 ♔d7 47.♖xc4 ♖b2, and Black wins the rook for the a-pawn and with it the game.
43...c4 44.♘f4 ♖a1+ 45.♔g2 a2!
The pawns decide!
46.♖a3 c3! 47.♘e2 c2 48.♔f2 ♖h1

Normally this is the winning idea without the e2-knight and the c2-pawn, but here it works just as effectively, as 49.♖xa2 is met with 49...♖xh2+ and 50...♖xe2!. White resigned.

■ ■ ■

Radjabov's new win suddenly put him in a position he could not have dreamed of a few days before: if he completed his hat-trick by beating Tomashevsky with the white pieces on the last day, he would qualify for the Candidates regardless of what happened in the other games. It sounded like a fairy-tale: Teimour Radjabov, who lost his place among the very best after a disastrous result at the 2013 London Candidates – where he had been given a wildcard because the event was sponsored with Azeri money – could reclaim his spot among the elite by winning his final game.

It was not to be. Radjabov arrived early for the game, fully concentrated and fully aware of the task before him, but he failed to break Rapport's resistance.

For MVL the situation was more complicated at the outset of the last round. Of course he depended on Radjabov's result, but of one thing he was certain: to keep his hopes alive he would have to win his own game. He didn't, and in the end he even lost.

NOTES BY
Anish Giri

Maxime Vachier-Lagrave
Dmitry Jakovenko
Mallorca 2017 (9)
Giuoco Piano

1.e4 e5 2.♘f3 ♘c6 3.♗c4 ♗c5 4.c3 ♘f6 5.d3 a6 6.0-0 d6 7.a4 ♗a7 8.♖e1 0-0 9.h3 h6 10.♘bd2 ♖e8

The best players have spent so many hours of their lives trying to understand all the differences between the various move orders that can lead to this position in the Italian Opening that I feel it would be irresponsible of me to explain it here to the readers.
11.b4 ♘e7 Strangely enough, this move had not yet been played in this position before. Perhaps the reason is that not many like to see their rook go back to f8 the next move.
11...♗e6 has been played against MVL a few times and I myself also have some experience in this position with the white pieces. White is generally very slightly better, essentially because of some extra space on the queenside and the 'bad' knight on c6. No big deal, though.
12.♕b3! Forcing the rook back to f8 can't be wrong.
12...♖f8

13.d4 The standard break in the centre. Most of us used to think that allowing the isolani with exd4

Palma de Mallorca 2017

					TPR
1	Levon Aronian	ARM	2801	5½	2742
2	Dmitry Jakovenko	RUS	2721	5½	2748
3	Hikaru Nakamura	USA	2780	5	2749
4	Ding Liren	CHN	2774	5	2729
5	Peter Svidler	RUS	2763	5	2745
6	Teimour Radjabov	AZE	2741	5	2723
7	Pentala Harikrishna	IND	2738	5	2728
8	Evgeny Tomashevsky	RUS	2702	5	2755
9	Richard Rapport	HUN	2692	5	2720
10	Maxime Vachier-Lagrave	FRA	2796	4½	2741
11	Pavel Eljanov	UKR	2707	4½	2729
12	Ernesto Inarkiev	RUS	2683	4½	2740
13	Anish Giri	NED	2762	4	2739
14	Li Chao	CHN	2741	4	2700
15	Paco Vallejo	ESP	2705	4	2727
16	Alexander Riazantsev	RUS	2651	3½	2725
17	Boris Gelfand	ISR	2719	3	2703
18	Jon Ludvig Hammer	NOR	2629	3	2712
18 players, 9 rounds					

cxd4 d5 is not good for White, but this opinion has slightly changed after Magnus Carlsen introduced this concept against Karjakin in the World Championship match. Apparently, White gets a lot of piece play, which Black fails to neutralize in every second game, despite his superior pawn structure.

13...exd4 13...♘g6 is a solid alternative. With the white queen far from the kingside, the thematic ...♘h7-♘g5 idea becomes ever more attractive for my *Fingerspitzengefühl*.

14.cxd4 d5 15.exd5 ♘exd5 16.b5

16...♗e6? Mixing up the move order, a common phenomenon at top level. It is only possible to play such an awful move when you are certain that it is what you had prepared at home. Otherwise for a player of Jakovenko's class and understanding such a giant strategic as well as tactical mistake is unthinkable.

16...axb5 17.axb5 ♗e6 is obviously stronger.

17.bxa6 White is, of course, happy to keep the a-pawns. Black's a6-pawn is extremely weak.

17...bxa6 18.♗a3 18.♘e5! at once was excellent as well. **18...♖e8**

19.♘e5! The knight is coming to c6. Black is in trouble.

19...♘f4 Black simplifies matters somewhat, the best way to go about things.

20.♘df3 Simple and strong. The eventual ♘c6 will define White's advantage. **20...♗xc4 21.♕xc4 ♕d5 22.♕xd5 ♘6xd5**

23.♘c6 23.a5 allows Black a brilliant regrouping: 23...♘c3! 24.♘c6 ♘b5!, with good chances to hold, although the a7-bishop vs c6-knight combo is really creepy for Black.

23...♖xe1+ 24.♖xe1 a5!
The only way to stay alive. Black now threatens to free the bishop with ...♗b6.

25.g3 ♘g6

26.♘xa7!? A very pretty idea, but the position gets somewhat simplified, and from a scientific point of view this might be inaccurate.

Better was 26.♘fe5! ♗b6 27.♘c4!, keeping the tension with a huge advantage. Black has no way to create any counterplay, and sooner or later White will get his rook around to b5 and pick up the a5-pawn.

26...♖xa7 27.♖e8+ ♔h7 28.h4!

Grand Prix 2017

					Sharjah	Moscow	Geneva	Mallorca	TOTAL
1	Shakhriyar Mamedyarov	IGM	AZE	2766	140	140	60		340
2	Alexander Grischuk	IGM	RUS	2742	140	71.⁴³	125		336.⁴³
3	Teimour Radjabov	IGM	AZE	2710		71.⁴³	170	71.⁴³	312.⁸⁶
4	Ding Liren	IGM	CHN	2760	70	170		71.⁴³	311.⁴³
5	Dmitry Jakovenko	IGM	RUS	2709	70		11	155	236
6	Maxime Vachier-Lagrave	IGM	FRA	2796	140	71.⁴³		20	231.⁴³
7	Hikaru Nakamura	IGM	USA	2785	70	71.⁴³		71.⁴³	212.⁸⁶
8	Peter Svidler	IGM	RUS	2748		71.⁴³	60	71.⁴³	202.⁸⁶
9	Ian Nepomniachtchi	IGM	RUS	2749	70	3	125		198
10	Levon Aronian	IGM	ARM	2785	7		11	155	173
11	Pentala Harikrishna	IGM	IND	2758		20	60	71.⁴³	151.⁴³
12	Anish Giri	IGM	NED	2769		71.⁴³	60	6	137.⁴³
13	Michael Adams	IGM	ENG	2751	70	3	60		133
14	Richard Rapport	IGM	HUN	2692	25		2.⁵⁰	71.⁴³	98.⁹³
15	Evgeny Tomashevsky	IGM	RUS	2711	3	20		71.⁴³	94.⁴³
16	Li Chao	IGM	CHN	2720	25		60	6	91
17	Hou Yifan	IGM	CHN	2651	7	71.⁴³	2.⁵⁰		80.⁹³
18	Alexander Riazantsev	IGM	RUS	2671	1		60	3	64
19	Pavel Eljanov	IGM	UKR	2759	25		11	20	56
20	Paco Vallejo	IGM	ESP	2709	25	7		6	38
21	Boris Gelfand	IGM	ISR	2720		20	11	1.⁵⁰	32.⁵⁰
22	Ernesto Inarkiev	IGM	RUS	2723		1	4	20	25
23	Jon Ludvig Hammer	IGM	NOR	2628	3	7		1.⁵⁰	11.⁵⁰
24	Salem Saleh	IGM	UAE	2656	3	3	1		7

Dmitry Jakovenko readily admitted that he had been lucky in the last round. Humorously, the Russian wished his colleagues similar luck in future events.

31.♔f1! ♘xa4 32.♔e2, bringing the king to the centre. In fact, White is still pressing.

31...♘xa4

32.♘e5!? A desperate decision to try and unsettle Black. 32.♘xa5 ♖b5 33.♖e5 c5 is a forced draw.

32...♘b6

When I first saw this position, I thought White should win, but then I spotted Black's answer when things get a little messy.

28...♖b7! 29.♘d2?

As Maxime admitted afterwards, he had forgotten about the fact that Black is in time to pick up the a-pawn now. And it's true that the d2-knight is way too far from the kingside.

Best was 29.♗c5!, but even here, if Black pulls himself together and finds some tough moves, the game is likely to still be within the drawing margins: 29...♖b3! 30.♘d2 ♖d3! 31.♘c4 h5! 32.♘xa5 ♘c3 33.♖c8 ♘xa4 34.♖xc7 f5!? 35.♘c4 f4 36.♔h2 fxg3+ 37.fxg3 ♘xc5 38.♖xc5 (38.dxc5 ♖c3) 38...♖xd4 39.♖xh5+ ♔g8, and this is the position that the computer is basing its high evaluation of the

position after 29.♗c5 on. True, White will push, but I don't think the result is much in doubt, when one faces as tough a defender as Jakovenko.

29...♘c3! 30.h5 ♘h8

Here the knight is OK for the time being. Now Maxime can obviously win the a5-pawn as well and try to milk something small, but the knight is likely to join in again after an eventual ...f6 and ...♘f7, with easy equality, so he tries to abandon the a-pawn and focus on domination. The idea in itself was OK, but the execution was not.

31.♘c4?!

After 31.♖a8 ♘xa4 32.♖xa5 ♘c3, followed by ...f6-...♘f7, as well as ...♖b5, the position is completely equal.

One way to keep the game going was

33.♗c5

It is hard for White to come up with a winning plan, since there is no such plan at all. It was probably best to leave the pawn on d4 and push the kingside pawns in hopes of some panic.

33...a4 34.d5 f6 35.♘c6

35...♘d7 Allowing White to get back into the game, but only with the idea of drawing it. Maxime wants to have none of it and eventually commits suicide.

35...♘xd5 was even stronger: 36.♘d4 ♘f7 37.♘e6 ♘g5 38.♘f8+ ♔g8, and there's no mate at all.

36.♗d4
36.♗e3 ♖b5 37.d6 cxd6 38.♖e7 ♘c5 39.♖a7 is fully equal, since White will win back a pawn and have enough positional compensation for the other one. Black is, of course, in no danger at all here.

36...♖b5

37.♘d8??
37.♖c8 ♖xd5 38.♖xc7 ♘f7 39.♗b2 was entirely within the drawing margins for White. It is a question of attitude, but for Maxime this game was all or nothing, so it makes no sense to blame him for not trying to fight for half a point.

37...♖b8

Taking on d5 was good too, but this is just lights out. The rest is agony.
38.♗b2 ♖xb2 39.♘e6 a3 40.♖e7 ♘f7 41.♖xf7 a2 42.♖xg7+ ♔h8 43.♖xd7 a1♕+ 44.♔g2 ♕e1
White resigned.

∎ ∎ ∎

Cruel blow of fate
Maxime Vachier-Lagrave's failure to qualify for Berlin was seen by many as a cruel blow of fate. The Frenchman had had three chances to realise his biggest dream – as he described qualifying for the Candidates in his recently published autobiographical book *Maxime Vachier-Lagrave, Joueur d'échecs* – and each time he had missed out by the narrowest of margins. In the end, he failed to qualify on rating, got knocked out of the World Cup in the semi-final and failed on the last day of the Grand Prix.

MVL himself tried to remain calm in the face of this bitter disappointment: 'I had estimated my chances to be 30%. I was pressing in a couple of games, but it didn't work out. Now I have to wait for two years, not

knowing if I will make it the next time. But I am not the only one, there are only eight places and Nakamura is not in either, nor is Vishy.'

The next series
For Dmitry Jakovenko, a second win and shared tournament victory were an unexpected windfall, although it was not the first time that he had beaten Vachier-Lagrave. The Russian's win, in fact, improved his overall score against MVL (not counting draws) to 5-0!

In a brief speech at the closing ceremony, Jakovenko admitted that he had been lucky, and humorously wished his colleagues similar luck in future events.

At the prize-giving, the CEO of World Chess, Ilya Merenzon, was absent, as he had been all through

the event. The next day he sent the players an email from London, where he was preparing the announcement of the 2018 World Championship match in the British capital. In his email, he urged the players to send in their reactions to the 2017 Grand Prix cycle: 'I am very keen to know how you liked the format (Swiss instead of Round Robin), fewer days (10 instead of 15) and the choice of cities. I would very much like to ask for your comments and feedback before we start planning the next Series.'

Ilyumzhinov's brainchild
The players' main concern may be the question of whether there will be a next series at all. The Grand Prix, after all, had been the brainchild of Kirsan Ilyumzhinov, the side-

'The players' main concern may be the question of whether there will be a next Grand Prix series at all.'

lined FIDE President, who had also found most of the mainly Russian sponsors. With Ilyumzhinov's future in the balance, that of the GP may have become uncertain as well. A tournament cycle with two spots in the Candidates at stake is attractive, but it would not be too complicated to select one more Candidate by rating and one more from the World Cup. So far, the public appeal of the Grand Prix has been almost negligible compared to the interest that the Candidates evokes (let alone the World Championship match), but there is much room for improvement, and it is a series of tournaments that makes sense. The players can only hope that it will remain part of the overall world championship cycle and that there will be another series. ∎

NEW IN CHESS bestsellers

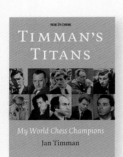

Timman's Titans
My World Champions
Jan Timman 320 pages - €26.95

ECF 2017 Book of the Year

"The book must be read to obtain the full flavour of Timman's writing (..) The most informative, interesting and revealing book on the world champions covered, both as people and chess players."
ECF Book of the Year Judges

Bologan's King's Indian
A Modern Repertoire for Black
Victor Bologan 368 pages - €29.95

In many lines Bologan presents two options to handle the Black position. With many new ideas and resources, and several offbeat sidelines that will enable you to surprise your opponent.

"Bologan's understanding of the King's Indian is second to few and here he maps out a pretty detailed repertoire for Black against all White's options." – *CHESS Magazine*

Training with Moska
Practical Chess Exercises: Tactics, Strategy, Endgames
Viktor Moskalenko 336 pages - €27.95

"A wonderful training manual. It will bring all players with an Elo of 1600 or more a strong improvement of their playing strength."
IM Dirk Schuh, Rochade Europa Magazine

"Another highly entertaining and instructive book (..) More books please, Moska!"
Sean Marsh, CHESS Magazine (UK)

The New In Chess Book of Chess Improvement
Lessons from the Best Players in the World's Leading Chess Magazine
Steve Giddins (editor) 336 pages - €22.95

Steve Giddins has arranged the most didactic annotations by the world's best players of the past three decades into thematic chapters.

"There is no doubt about it: the games and annotations really are top-notch and any player studying the material would definitely improve various aspects of their own play."
Sean Marsh, CHESS Magazine (UK)

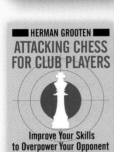

Chess for Hawks
Improve your vision, sharpen your talons, forget your fear
Cyrus Lakdawala 288 pages - €22.95

WINNER: Best Instructional Book
Chess Journalists of America

"A very good manual for those who feel they got stuck at a certain level and can't quite find the way to break through to the next level."
Carsten Hansen, author of 'The Chameleon Variation'

Chess Training for Candidate Masters
Accelerate Your Progress by Thinking for Yourself
Alexander Kalinin 208 pages - €18.95

"Sasha Kalinin has an acute understanding of what modern chess players struggle with and what they must do in order to improve." – *GM Daniel Naroditsky*

"Kalinin writes that the target audience of his book is up to about 2200 Elo in rating, but it embraces much more than that. It is a good book for both club players AND grandmasters!" – *GM Simen Agdestein, VG Daily Newspaper*

Attacking Chess for Club Players
Improve Your Skills to Overpower Your Opponents
Herman Grooten 352 pages - €27.95

Third, improved & extended edition

"A really stimulating book with quite original ideas in how to develop the skills that we need when we're attacking. Not only very instructive, but really good fun as well."
GM Daniel King

"Succeeds and amuses, and is truly suitable for players of all levels." – *IM Frank Zeller, SCHACH Magazine*

The Berlin Defence Unraveled
A Straightforward Guide for Black and White
Luis Bernal 272 pages - €27.95

Finally: the Berlin + the Anti-Berlin for Club Players!

"The claim of 'unraveling' the Berlin is completely justified. An extremely instructive and clear-cut work."
Der Neue Tag Newspaper

"Bernal investigates the latest theoretical developments, but hasn't skimped on explanation." – *GM Glenn Flear*

My First Chess Opening Repertoire for White / for Black
A Ready-to-go Package for Ambitious Beginners
Vincent Moret 240 pages - €19.95

"I would expect the recommended lines to grow in popularity at club level and they would make an excellent surprise weapon in tournament play too." – *CHESS Magazine*

"This book is filled with exciting, tactical lines."
Jeremy Silman, chess.com

"Will definitely improve your rating."
IM Gary Lane, ECF Newletter

Endgame Tactics
A Comprehensive Guide to the Sunny Side of Chess Endgames – New, Improved and Expanded Edition
Van Perlo 608 pages - €29.95

WINNER: ECF Book of the Year Award
WINNER: ChessCafe Book of the Year Award

" It cannot but help to improve your chess, painlessly, enjoyably." – *Chess Today*

"A masterpiece." – *Former US Champion Joel Benjamin*

available at your local (chess)bookseller or at www.newinchess.com

SHORT

DON'T SPOIL THE FUN

This year marks the centenary of Marcel Duchamp's controversial 'Fountain' – a porcelain urinal submitted for an exhibition of the Society of Independent Artists at the Grand Central Palace in New York. Depending on one's degree of pretentiousness or cynicism, this was either a defining moment in the history of 20th century art or, as the committee which rejected it probably concluded, a flagrant piss-take – quite literally so, in this case.

By coincidence, I was once presented with an official Duchamp-estate miniature of this iconic masterpiece when I met the late artist's widow, Teeny Duchamp, at a tournament in the 1980s. For a while this was mounted proudly and appropriately enough in our W.C. until one day, after returning from a foreign excursion, I could find it no more. Inquiring of my wife where the provocative *objet d'art* had gone, she admitted to having thrown it out in revulsion. Disregarding the fact that it was worth at least several hundred euros at the time, or several thousand in today's money, even had it been a mere tuppenny trinket, she had absolutely no right to toss away a gift of mine without seeking permission. Alas, such painful, tragic tribulations – unknown to the single man – are the flip side of married life.

Duchamp had a healthy chess addiction and was good enough to represent France, behind Alekhine, at the Hamburg Olympiad in 1930 – drawing with the legendary Frank Marshall in the first round. He famously flattered our fraternity with the quote 'While all artists are not chess players, all chess players are artists'. Like much of modern art, this pleasing pronouncement is little more than utter rubbish disguised as profundity. Many devotees of Caïssa are, of course, crass, uncultured philistines who would not recognise a thing of beauty if it poked them in the eye.

I was forcibly reminded of this recently at the Negros International Open in Bacolod City in the Philippines. Despite winning outright with 8/9, I somehow avoided playing most of the top-seeds. In the seventh round, no less, I found myself in the highly unusual situation of facing an unrated opponent on Board 1 – the originally-named Danmaersk Mangao. I later asked him whether his father was a sailor, to which he replied 'Yes, how did you know?' Just a wild stab in the dark, on my part... Anyway, to return to the story, after 23 moves we reached the following position:

After an excessively long think, during which time I joked to the organisers that my opponent was perhaps hoping that I would die of a heart-attack before his flag

> ### 'This pleasing pronouncement is little more than utter rubbish disguised as profundity.'

fell, my antagonist had tried his last desperate roll of the dice, 23...♕h5-h7, optimistically dreaming of delivering checkmate on c2. White now has the glorious, exceptionally rare, and, who knows, possibly even unprecedented opportunity to win a miniature with a double consecutive under-promotion: 24.f8♘+! ♖xf8 25.g7xf8♘+!. Please note that the first under-promotion is the strongest move and the second, far from being gratuitous, is the only move not to lose. However, confused by the latest FIDE rule changes, I was unsure whether a procedurally incorrect promotion might lead to me being forfeited (only in Rapid or Blitz, but not Classical chess, apparently) and so I took a second or two to carefully pick up a knight in my right hand in anticipation of executing the killing combination. Unfortunately, before I could physically complete the move, my opponent, to my absolute dismay, had rushed forward in an orgasm of resignation.

STORIES

How dare he spoil my exquisite, artistic creation? What a wanton act of aesthetic sabotage! I started to protest, but the arbiter had by now stepped in, stopped the clock and was demanding signatures.

Such spoilsport, party-pooping antics, in a selfish desire to avoid perceived humiliation, are, alas, not uncommon. Minutes before I began this article, I stumbled across a fresh tweet by David Llada in which he lauded Laurent Fressinet for a brilliancy in Barcelona, but almost audibly sighed 'it is a pity his opponent resigned immediately' before the Frenchman could uncork his second bishop sacrifice. Indeed. It is like watching football, but without the goals. With such aesthetic vandalism we cut ourselves off from our current fan base and build a veritable Berlin Wall of exclusion against millions of potential devotees. Not everyone who knows how to move the pieces is capable of calculating lengthy combinations (far from it) and we do them a deep disservice by denying them a fitting finish. When so much of chess is humdrum and routine, why is it considered acceptable, by so many, to ruin the beauty we have?

I suspect the answer is that the converse sin – the late resignation – is, arguably, an even greater scourge. Early in our chess careers we are taught that it is impolite to play on in completely lost positions. Most people grasp the concept well enough, although obviously weaker players tend to be slower in appreciating their abject plight. The key point here though is the hopelessness: there is nothing reprehensible at all in continuing a bad or even lost position if the tiniest glimmer of light still flickers. Chess is a fight, after all. But when that hope is extinguished, and nothing but irksome drudgery remains, the decent thing to do is resign and not waste everyone's time. Do not, under any circumstances, sit there for ages, as Hikaru Nakamura did against Fabiano Caruana earlier this year, petulantly wallowing in self-pity and not moving. That is ungentlemanly. Normally though, it is usually only in the socially competitive arenas, such as simuls, that one finds oneself checkmating opponents with an overwhelming material superiority. No matter how often people are informed 'there are no prizes for being last to finish', the lure of bragging rights is invariably too strong for some people to resist. Alas, a poor tune with many notes is in no way superior to a poor tune with few notes – rather the opposite, in fact.

It is not only decisive games that sometimes dawdle to tedious conclusions, draws do too. One of the great innovations of recent years has been the introduction of the Sofia Rules, which has dealt a mighty blow to, if not quite eradicated, the blight of the so-called 'grandmaster draw'. Revolutionary in its time, the prohibition on early agreed handshakes has nowadays become so commonplace in major tournaments that it is hardly ever questioned. And that is a very good thing. At the risk of tautology, the point of a game of chess is to play chess. But while there has been a most welcome gain in combativeness, the (minor but nevertheless real)

'With such aesthetic vandalism we cut ourselves off from our current fan base.'

downside has been an increase in plodding monotony. Positions that would have been abandoned as sterile in former years, and which, quite frankly, ought to be euthanized, must now lumber ponderously to their inevitable end, to the edification of no one.

The call for creativity is often the pathetic refrain of aging has-beens whose results have gone to pot. The last thing your columnist would want is to be compared to David Bronstein, whose excruciating biography ('Decline & Decline' I call it) by Genna Sosonko I recently read. Incidentally, I finally understood why I could not abide talking to him, despite holding him in great admiration. No, chess is a sport and results should always be paramount.

The aim of this article is more modest – just to remind people what attracted us to chess in the first place. Obviously not because it was a smart career move or – as the latest faddists would have us believe – that it was a valuable tool in education. For me, at least, it was because, at its best, it is a game of sublime beauty. And if the only price we need to pay for sharing in that collective joy is by showing a little over-the-board courtesy, or by allowing our opponents to demonstrate their artistry, it is not too much to ask, is it?

Nigel Short

Azerbaijan pips Russia to the post

European Team Championship decided by smallest of margins

FIDE Deputy President Giorgios Makropoulos congratulates Mahir Mamedov and Faik Hasanov, Azmaiparashvili watches the moment with members of the winning team: (l to r.) Rauf Mamedov

Unruffled by a sensational first-round loss, Azerbaijan went on to win the European Team Championship in a classic comeback story. The key match was the Azeris' 3-1 win against top favourites Russia. Their top-performer was Rauf Mamedov, who scored an incredible 8 from 9. In the women's section, the Russian squad did live up to expectations. Led by former World Champion Alexandra Kosteniuk, they claimed the title with one round to spare. **ERWIN L'AMI** reports from Crete.

The Creta Maris Beach Resort in Hersonissos, on Greece's largest island, Crete, is a familiar destination for many chess players. Over the years it has been the venue for quite a few competitions organized by the European Chess Union and FIDE. For me, as a member of the Dutch team, the 2017 European Team Chess Championship (ETCC) meant my third visit, and I talked to colleagues who (in total) had spent months there! The resort, overlooking the Bay of Malia, is excellent, and even at the end of October the weather is still very pleasant.

My previous visit had been for the ETCC of 2007, exactly 10 years ago, and I recall that I escaped with

Vice-Presidents of the Azerbaijan Chess Federation, European Chess Union, President Zurab

a draw against Rauf Mamedov in our match against Azerbaijan. Rauf, 19 years old at the time, had already established his reputation as an online blitz monster and could be found on the ICC at any time of the day. In the years that followed, he became a fixture on the Azeri team and established his rating in the 2650-2690 range. The big leap forward, however, never came – until

'But to say that Azerbaijan's victory was plain sailing could not be further from the truth.'

the European Team Championship of this year. Rather than the stars Shakhriyar Mamedyarov, Teimour Radjabov or Arkadij Naiditsch, it was largely Board 4, Rauf Mamedov, who led the Azeri team to victory in Crete. Since he scored an astonishing 8 out of 9, the others only needed to 'hold' their boards, which everybody duly did.

But to say that their victory was plain sailing could not be further from the truth. In the first round, Azerbaijan, seeded second, suffered a sensational defeat against Italy. In fact, the Italians, seeded only 22nd, won remarkably easily. But this upset apparently shocked the Azeri into the right frame of mind, and we witnessed a classic comeback story! Before that story unfolds, however, let's first widen our perspective a bit.

Before each big team event, Russia are usually the clear favourites, and this time was not an exception. Even without Vladimir Kramnik and Sergey Karjakin, their team captain Alexander Motylev was spoiled for choice! The Russians got off to a convincing start, winning their first three matches. From those early rounds I'd like to single out a typically powerful win by Ian Nepomniachtchi, against Viktor Laznicka of the Czech Republic.

Ian Nepomniachtchi
Viktor Laznicka
Hersonissos 2017 (3)
Caro-Kann, Advance Variation

1.e4 c6 2.d4 d5 3.e5 ♗f5 4.♘f3 e6 5.♗e2 c5
Laznicka has a pretty tight repertoire, and this can be a liability against a team like Russia. The Russians always have plenty of seconds on site

who tend to come up with excellent ideas in the openings. This game is no exception.

6.♗e3 cxd4 7.♘xd4 ♘e7
One can find about a dozen of Laznicka's games from this exact position.
8.0-0 ♘bc6 9.♗b5 a6 10.♗xc6+ bxc6 11.c4 ♕d7

12.♘c3
12.cxd5 ♘xd5 13.♘xf5 exf5 14.♗d4

♖b8 is very fine for Black, as practice has shown. The knight will usually reroute to the beautiful e6-square.
12...dxc4 13.♘a4 ♘d5 14.♗xf5 exf5 15.♖c1 c3

16.♕c2!? A very serious new idea. 16.♘xc3 ♘xe3 17.fxe3 g6, as in Caruana-Navara, Baku 2016, is less worrying for Black.
16...♗e7
I like it that nowadays the time spent on each move is stored as well, which provides useful information if you follow the games live or play through them afterwards. Here Black spent 21 minutes, and this was basically his first real think of the game. 16...cxb2 is the critical reply, but one can understand Laznicka's reluctance to go down this path. A sample line showing the dangers is 17.♕xb2 f4 (17...♗e7 18.e6!?) 18.♘c5 ♗xc5 19.♗xc5 f3 20.♖c4!, stopping Black's counterplay and leaving the king stranded in the middle of the board.
17.♘xc3 ♘xe3 18.fxe3

Here White has a much improved version of the above-mentioned Caruana-Navara game. The reason why will become clear shortly.

18...♗g5 19.♖ce1 g6
Nepomniachtchi also started taking his time around here, indicating the game had now really 'started'. I was impressed by the powerplay that followed.

20.g4! Just before Black gets his king to safety, White strikes.
20...fxg4 21.♘e4 Again with tempo. **21...♗e7 22.♖d1 ♕c8 23.e6** I'm not going to criticize this move too much, because it will win the game in just a few moves. Moreover, it screams out to be played. Yet, Black now misses a good fighting chance, so the less spirited 23.♘c5 was the better option, when after 23...0-0 (23...♖xc5 24.♕xc5 is pretty hopeless with the king on e8) 24.♘d7, Black falls apart as 24...♖d8 is solidly met by 25.e6 (25...fxe6 26.♕e4).

23...fxe6?? Collapsing under the immense pressure. The forced line 23...♕xe6 24.♘d6+ ♗xd6 25.♕xc6+ ♔f8 (or 25...♔e7 26.♕b7+ ♔f8 27.♕xa8+, transposing) 26.♕xa8+ ♔g7 27.♕d5 ♕xd5 28.♖xd5 ♗e7! leads to an endgame in which Black may just be perfectly OK. **24.♕c3** The queen entering signals the imme-

Rauf Mamedov was the cornerstone of the Azeri team, scoring an unbelievable 8 out of 9 (performance rating 2920!), and contributing a brilliant win in the key match against Russia.

diate collapse. **24...♖f8 25.♖xf8+ ♗xf8 26.♕h8** Black resigned, since there is no stopping ♘d6+.

Meanwhile, Azerbaijan had dropped another match point when they drew with Spain, 2-2. As a result, they lingered in shared 18th place and had every reason to be dissatisfied. But from here on in, things started changing... To begin with, they took out Moldova 4-0 in Round 4.

Andrei Macovei
Rauf Mamedov
Hersonissos 2017 (4)

position after 41...h5

Take all the major pieces off and a draw can be agreed on the spot. However, that is never going to

happen. Given the inactivity of the white bishop, I'd say that Black's advantage is already likely to be of a winning nature, but he could still have put up a stiff defence with 41.g3, to cover the dark squares. Macovei tried something similar with **41.h4**, only to get hit by **41...♖a2!**

42.♕e1 (because 42.♕xa2 ♕xh4+ is mate in 3), and now the excruciating **42...♔g7**. It turns out that White is paralyzed. Illustrative is the line 43.♖g1 ♖b2 44.g3, intending to go ♖g2 next move, but now 44...♕xh4+! forces mate. After the further **43.♗d3 ♖b2 44.♗c4 ♗c3 45.♕g3 ♕xe4 46.♗d3 ♕e7** White had seen enough. A nice example of the relative strength of opposite-coloured bishops.

In the same round that Azerbaijan started their resurgence, the Russian team took their first blow. The encounter with Hungary saw three games drawn, while Viktor Erdös defeated Ian Nepomniachtchi in exemplary fashion.

The surprise leaders after five rounds were Croatia, captained by former European Champion Zdenko Kozul. Their hero, Marin Bosiocic, went on to score 6/8, and his 2824 performance was the best result on Board 2. Before you look at the following position, you may cover the text following the diagram and treat it as a tactical test. Bosiocic was Black and his German opponent, Matthias Blübaum, had two king moves at his disposal. Which one would you choose?

Matthias Blübaum
Marin Bosiocic
Hersonissos 2017 (5)

position after 34...♖g6+

The move that had to be played was 35.♔h1!, not fearing any ghosts along the long diagonal. However, Blübaum picked the other square, **35.♔f1** and after **35...♗e6! 36.fxe3 ♗d8!! 37.e4 ♗h3+ 38.♔f2 ♗h4+** he lost a rook in broad daylight!

It took the force of Hungary to stop Croatia in Round 6. With an in-form Peter Leko on Board 1 and both Erdös and Richard Rapport doing excellent jobs on Boards 2 and 3, the Hungarians looked set for a medal. However, by Round 7, Azerbaijan had returned to the top and defeated Hungary 3-1.

The key match that essentially decided the championship came in Round 8, the penultimate round. After their slip-up against Hungary, Russia had made no further mistakes, and won all their matches. Azerbaijan was trailing by one match point, and now they met in a direct encounter.

Board 1 saw an epic clash between Alexander Grischuk and Shakhriyar Mamedyarov. Following the classic Kortchnoi-Portisch from Wijk aan Zee 1968, Shakh was taking no prisoners as he repeated the move ...g7-g5 in the generally quiet variation of the Neo-Steinitz in the Ruy Lopez. Grischuk was caught off-guard and Anish Giri takes us through the game!

NOTES BY
Anish Giri

Alexander Grischuk
Shakhriyar Mamedyarov
Hersonissos 2017 (8)
Ruy Lopez, Neo-Steinitz Variation

1.e4 e5 2.♘f3 ♘c6 3.♗b5 a6 4.♗a4
Shakhriyar has struggled in the main lines of the Spanish before when facing Alexander Grischuk's forceful 1.e4 service, and here he decides to use one of his old favourites, the Neo-Steinitz. Also a favourite of Eltaj Safarli – the coach of the Azeris.
4...d6 5.0-0 ♗d7

6.♖e1 A clever move, but it meets with an even cleverer reply. White's point is to economize on the c3-move.

A rapid game Kasimdzhanov-Mamedyarov, Almaty 2016, saw 6.c3 g6 (6...g5, as played in the game, makes less sense here: 7.d4 g4 8.♘e1) 7.d4 ♗g7 8.♗e3 ♘f6 9.♘bd2 ♘g4 10.♗g5 f6 11.♗h4 ♕e7 12.♖e1 h5 13.h3 ♘h6 14.♗g3 g5 15.♘f1 0-0-0 (0-1, 37).
6...g5!? A shocker, but a little less so if you know that it is the computer's first choice. Perhaps Grischuk didn't take it seriously.
6...g6 7.d4!? ♗g7 8.d5 ♘ce7 9.c4 in one go is the point.

7.♗xc6 7.d4 g4 is likely to transpose, but 8.d5!? is an extra option here.
7...bxc6 8.d4 g4 9.♘fd2 exd4 10.♘b3 10.♘c4!? is more cunning.
10...♘e7 11.♘xd4 ♗g7 12.♘c3 0-0 Black has finished his development and enjoys the bishop pair, while the weaknesses on the kingside are hardly felt.

13.♗g5?! Provoking ...f6 is wrong, strangely enough. Black will be happy to get ...♕e8-g6 in.
13.♗e3!? was stronger, but we can't speak of any problems for Black. The theoreticians won't spend much time here and will do their research somewhere between moves 5 and 10.

13...f6 14.♗e3

f4 is a better square for the bishop, as we will later see. For instance 14...♕e8 15.♕d2 ♕g6.

14...♕e8! 15.♕d3 ♕f7 16.♕d2 ♕g6

17.♗f4

Grischuk struggles to find a good plan. Going for b4 and a4 does not seem correct. Instead, it was best to go f3 or f4 here or on the next move. White will stop Black's easy plan of ...h5-h4-h3 and should be able to get an unclear game going. Still, at this point Black's position should be slightly preferred, thanks to his bishop pair.

17...h5 18.b4?!

As mentioned above, this plan turns out to be a waste of time. White will anyway get distracted by the action on the kingside and the a4-b4-pawns are going to be left hanging in the air. 18.f3! was still best.

18...h4!

A natural plan to develop an initiative on the kingside.

19.a4 ♕h5 20.♗e3 h3 21.♘ce2

21.g3 is ugly: 21...f5!.

21...hxg2 22.♘f4

The day of truth, Russia-Azerbaijan. Ian Nepomniachtchi shakes hands with Teimour Radjabov, while Grischuk and Mamedyarov prepare for a memorable battle on Board 1.

The g2-pawn would serve White as a good protective shield, but the problem is that the e7-knight will find its way to f3, when things will get nasty for White's king.

22...♕h7 22...♕f7 was also possible. In fact, Black has plenty of nice options on every move. His position is just very good.

23.♘fe6 ♗xe6 24.♘xe6

24...♘g6!

Black wastes no time, as he clearly will be able to get the exchange back once the knight lands on f3. In a couple of moves' time, Grischuk collapses, which is not surprising, given how unpleasant his position is.

25.♘xf8 ♖xf8

Black has the easy plan of getting his knight to f3, going ...f5 at some point and then trying to finish off the attack. White is practically unable to stop it, but the machine still finds a way to kind of keep things together.

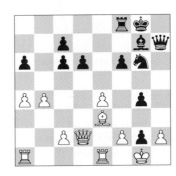

26.♗f4?

This loses. Best was 26.♖a3!, preparing to sacrifice the exchange on f3: 26...f5 27.♗d4 (27.exf5 ♗e5!

28.♗h6 ♖xf5 wins for Black) 27...f4
28.♗xg7 ♕xg7 29.f3!

ANALYSIS DIAGRAM

This still looks horrible for White, but
it seems that with computer precision
he can hold here. Black obviously can
win back the exchange at any time,
but things are likely to get simplified
then.

26...f5 27.exf5 ♘h4 28.♖a3

28.♕d3 is quite resilient, but Black
wins by force in study-like fashion:
28...♗xa1 29.♖xa1 ♘f3+ 30.♔xg2
♖f6! 31.♕e4 (31.♗g3 ♕h3+ 32.♔h1
♖h6 33.♕c4+ ♔f8 34.♕f4 comes
down to the same thing) 31...♔f8!
32.♗g3 ♕h3+ 33.♔h1 ♖h6 34.♕f4

ANALYSIS DIAGRAM

And here it is important to realize
that Black wins once he gets his rook
to the e-file threatening ...♖e1+! ♖xe1
♘xe1, with ...♕g2 and ...♕f1 checkmate coming. Then the solution
becomes easy: 34...♖h7! 35.f6 ♖h5!
36.f7 ♖h6!, and there is no stopping
...♖e6 (after 36...♖e5 White would
have 37.♕f6!).

**28...♕xf5 29.♗g5 ♘f3+ 30.♖xf3
gxf3 31.♗h6**

31...♕d5?

A lapse at the end, but Shakh gets
away with it.

31...♕f6! 32.♗xg7 ♔xg7 wins, as
Black will eventually get to either the
h2-pawn or the first rank.

32.♕c1?

Here 32.♕e3!! could have led to a
miraculous escape: 32...♗d4 33.♕e7
♖f5

ANALYSIS DIAGRAM

34.c4!! (if 34.♕d8+ then 34...♔h7
35.♕h4 ♖e5! 36.♖xe5 ♗xe5 wins,
as Black escapes the perpetual check
brilliantly: 37.♗d2+ ♔g8 38.♕g5+
♔f7 39.♕f5+ ♔e8 40.♕c8+ ♔e7
41.♕xc7+ ♔f6, and now, after giving
up the c7-pawn, Black goes back
again: 42.♕d8+ ♔g6 43.♕g5+ ♔f7
44.♕f5+ ♔e7 45.♗g5+ – 45.♕g5+
♔d7 – 45...♔e8 46.♕g6+ ♔d7
47.♕f5+, and now it helps that the
c7-pawn is gone: 47...♔c7!) 34...♗xf2+
(34...♕xc4 35.♕h4!) 35.♔xf2 ♕d4+
36.♗e3 ♕b2+ 37.♔g3! f2 38.♕e6+
♖f7 39.♕c8+ ♔h7 40.♕h3+ I don't
really know what to say.

32...♗c3!

Now Black wins. The queen ending
with the pawn on g2 is hopeless for
White.

33.♖e3

After 33.♖d1, 33...♕h5! 34.♗xf8
♗e5! hurts: 35.h3 ♕xh3, and Black
runs away from the checks quickly
(35...♔xf8!? is easier actually):
36.♕g5+ ♔xf8 37.♕d8+ ♔f7
38.♕xc7+ ♔g8 39.♕d8+ ♔h7
40.♕e7+ ♔g7 41.♕e4+ ♔g8 42.♕e8+
♗f8 43.♕g6+ ♔h8 44.♕f6+ ♔g7
45.♕d8+ ♔h7. And after 33.♗xf8
♗xe1 34.♕xe1 ♔xf8 Black wins
automatically.

**33...♗d4 34.♖d3 ♖e8 35.c3
♗xf2+ 36.♔xf2 ♖e2+**

The problem is that after ...♕xd3,
♕g5+ ♔f7, White runs out of checks
pretty quickly, so he resigned.

■ ■ ■

Perhaps even more impressive was
Rauf Mamedov's dominating win
over Daniil Dubov. Relying on deep
opening preparation, Mamedov
steered the game straight from the
opening into an endgame in which
White was a piece down but had
tremendous long-term compensation. Anish Giri answers the question
of whether Dubov could have saved
the game somewhere along the way.

NOTES BY
Anish Giri

Rauf Mamedov
Daniil Dubov
Hersonissos 2017 (8)
Sicilian Defence, Rossolimo Attack

1.e4 c5 2.♘f3 ♘c6 3.♗b5

Daniil Dubov and Rauf Mamedov are big experts of the Rossolimo Sicilian, and since both teams, Russia and Azerbaijan, were supported by some heavy theoreticians in Crete, a theoretical battle was bound to take place.
3...g6 4.0-0!?
4.♗xc6 is traditionally the main line, in which lately the focus has shifted to the sharp variations beginning with 4...bxc6.
4...♗g7 5.♖e1 ♘f6
Another direction would be 5...e5. A recent high-level game saw a bizarre sequence of moves after this, unlikely to be seen in one of the main lines of modern chess theory: 6.b4!? cxb4 7.a3 b3!? 8.cxb3 ♘ge7, Bacrot-Grischuk, Paris Rapid 2017 (0-1, 48).
6.e5 ♘d5 7.♘c3 ♘c7 8.♗xc6 dxc6
Here, taking with the b-pawn would be less attractive, as becomes clear once you start comparing the variations with those arising from 4.♗xc6 bxc6.
9.♘e4
Still a major theoretical line so far, but one which has remained in the shadow of the main variations in this opening. Black is at a crossroads again.

9...b6
This allows a check on f6, stripping the black king of his right to castle.
9...♗e6 is more natural when it comes to king safety, but Black's position loses a lot of its dynamism once the c8-bishop is shut out and the c7-knight has determined its placement. Plenty of high-level games have been played here and will no doubt be played in the future.
10.♘f6+
Critical.
10...♔f8 11.♘e4 ♗g4
The advantage of 9...b6: Black immediately puts pressure on the e5-pawn.
12.d3 ♗xe5?!
A rare move, and for a good reason. The following pseudo queen sac leads

to a very scary position for Black. According to Grischuk, who was caught in a talkative mood in the studio after the game, this had been advised by Boris Gelfand. A rare instance of two great theoreticians of our times having their sense of danger betray them.
More common than the move in the game is 12...♘e6.
And 12...♗h5 was seen in Mamedov-Vakhidov, Moscow 2017: 13.h3 ♗xf3 14.♕xf3 h6 15.a4 a5 16.♘d2 ♘e6 17.♘c4 ♕c7 18.c3 (1-0, 48).

13.♘xe5! ♗xd1 14.♘h6+ ♔g8
15.♘xc6 ♗xc2

16.♘xc5!?
Besides an ancient game between Jan Timman and a rather young Vladimir Kramnik, there weren't many high-level sources here. Rauf

> '**According to Grischuk this had been advised by Boris Gelfand. A rare instance of two great theoreticians of our times to have their sense of danger betray them.**'

plays a spectacular novelty, but in fact it was just as good to first take on d8, which in fact was the move order chosen in some non-human games.
16.♘c3 was seen in the aforementioned ancient game, when White wins an exchange, but with two pawns for it Black appears to be doing alright. I suspect this must have been the main focus of Dubov's and Gelfand's preparation. Timman-Kramnik, Riga 1995, continued: 16...e6 17.♘xd8 ♖xd8 18.♗g5 ♔g7 19.♗xd8 ♖xd8 20.♖ac1 ♗xd3

21.♖ed1 e5 22.♖e1 ♖e8 23.b3 ♘b5, and in those days it was normal to call it a day once both sides felt the position was somewhat simplified and equal. Draw.

16...bxc5 17.♘xd8 ♖xd8 18.♖xe7 ♘e6 The best square for the knight. **19.♖e1**

Taking on a7 was an option too, but mobilizing the last piece makes sense. This is a good moment to pause and philosophize about the position, as calculating it till the very end

appears to be pretty difficult, even for the strongest chess engines. To begin with, White is always able to take on e6 and make a draw with the ♖g7-xh7-g7-h7 sequence. This is probably what Dubov assumed would be the way this game was going to end. On the other hand, White is in no hurry to do so, unless Black is about to disturb White's bishop on h6, which locks up the king on g8 and the rook on h8, making sure White is virtually an exchange up rather than a piece down.

...♘g7, with the idea of going ...♘f5, is always met by g2-g4!, and Black's only other idea is to harass the e7-rook and eventually prepare ...f6 and ...♔f7. This is what Daniil attempts to do.

19...♗a4?!

I would attach a question mark to this move, since Black's idea fails to yield him a forced draw. But I am a little bit worried that the position could already be bad for Black anyway.

19...a6 is very logical, to not let White create a passed pawn, and there was one non-human game that ended in a draw here. But in fact White can win a pawn here by force: 20.b3! ♗xd3 21.♖d1 c4. The only move, otherwise ♖xd3 was a major threat (in case of 21...♘g7, White's pawn push to g4 can be met by ...♖d4 and. ..♗b5, so the cleanest is just the prophylactic 22.f4!? ♘f5 23.♖xd3, and now, no matter where the black rook will go, White will get out of the fork with tempo: 23...♖b8 24.♖b7!). 22.bxc4 ♖b8, and here the computer catches up with me and takes over, when he suddenly offers 23.f3!? ♗xc4 24.a4 and claims that Black is busted. There are too many open files for White to finally create a mating threat on the back rank, I guess.

19...♗xd3!? could be the best attempt. The point is that 20.♖xa7 can be met by 20...♘d4!?, when g4 is no longer possible due to ...♘f5, and ♖ae7 can

be met by ...♗b5. White doesn't have to take on a7, but then he will have to think how to break through, and again there is the idea of ...♗b5 and ...♘d4. This may hold, but I don't make any promises. For example, White can go a4!? somewhere, stopping ...♗b5, when Black will have to come up with a different plan to rescue his cornered kingside.

20.♖xa7 ♗c6

20...♗d7, with the idea of ...f6, is met by 21.♖e5!.

Faced by Rauf Mamedov's spectacular novelty, Daniil Dubov realizes that it's going to be a tough afternoon. Valentina Gunina and Ian Nepomniachtchi do not look too optimistic either.

21.h4

In fact, the sequence 21...♖a8 22.♖xe6 fxe6 23.♖c7 e5! is going to happen no matter what, so in anticipation of that, the computer comes up with the move 21.f3!?, preparing to bring the king closer to the action at the end of this exchange operation.

21...♖a8

22.♖xe6!?

Forcing matters. White also had a couple of other seductive options. For instance: 22.♖xa8+!? ♗xa8 23.♖e5! (an important prophylactic move – after 23.g4 ♗d5 24.f4 f6 25.f5 ♔f7 Black equalizes) 23...♗c6 24.d4!

cxd4 25.b4, and Black still struggles to come up with a constructive plan to rescue his h8-rook, while the white queenside pawns are going to be storming down the board.

The indecisive 22.♖e7!? shouldn't be met by 22...♖e8, but 22...♘d4!? seems to offer some hope.

22...fxe6 23.♖c7!

A brilliant move. In fact, this is a positional rook sacrifice! I can easily imagine that unarmed spectators were expecting a perpetual check instead.

23...♖d8?

A mistake! Black should have dug deep here and realized what the position is about. Only then is it possible to come up with the best solution.

23...♗d5 is natural, but weak. White just pushes his a-pawn. and there is nothing Black can do besides giving back a full rook: 24.a4 ♖xa4 25.♖g7+ ♔f8 26.♖a7+ ♔e8 27.♖xa4, and White is technically winning.

The only defence was the prophylactic(!) 23...e5!. Black prepares for ♖xc6, and although White has a move now to prepare for ...♖d8, there isn't anything spectacular he can do. The main line goes 24.a3 ♖d8. Preparing ...♗d7. Now White is forced to pick up the bishop: 25.♖g7+! ♔f8 26.♖xg6+ ♔f7 27.♖xc6 ♖c8, and White has 3(!) pawns for the exchange, but it seems that Black's chances of saving this game are very real here. In any case, this is certainly a huge improvement compared to the game.

23...♖e8 prepares ...♔f7 after ♖xc6, but is something of a wasted tempo. White is not going to take the bishop

just yet and just plays 24.♔f1!?.
24.♖xc6 Only a temporary relief for Black. **24...♔f7**

25.♖c7+! The key check. Black's king is forced back to the 8th rank.
25...♔e8 Here the king stands better than on g8, but with only an exchange down, White is soon going to be up material after he picks up the remaining weak pawns.
26.♗g5! ♖b8 27.♖e7+ ♔f8 28.♗f6 ♖a8 29.a3 h5
Clever, but Black is going to be material down and have a hopeless task ahead of him anyway.
30.♖c7 ♖g8 31.f4 ♔e8 32.♔f2 ♖b8 33.♗e5 ♖b3 34.♔e3 ♔d8 35.♖xc5 White first improves his position to the max and only then takes the abandoned c5-pawn.
35...♖b7 36.♗c3 ♖a7 37.♗b4 ♔d7

Black has finally reached some kind of harmony and coordination, but by now he is simply too many pawns down. White has various methods of winning and Rauf eventually finished the job. The rest of the game is a technical job, and I am not sure there is much to say about it. As long as

White does sensible things, sooner or later he should just win.
38.♖g5 ♔c6 39.♔e4 ♖f7 40.♖c5+ ♔b6 41.♖e5 ♖e8 42.♗a5+ ♔c6 43.♗c3 ♖f5 44.g3 ♔d7 45.♖a5 ♖xa5 46.♗xa5

White either promotes his queenside pawns or gets to the g6-pawn and promotes the kingside pawns...
46...♖a8 47.♗b4 ♖c8 48.♗c3 ♖a8 49.♔e5 ♖a6 50.♔f6 ♖d6 51.♔xg6 ♖xd3 52.♔xh5 ♖xg3 53.a4 ♔c6 54.♗e5 ♖g1 55.♔h6 ♖a1 56.h5 ♖xa4 57.♔g6 ♖a1 58.♗f6

The h-pawn runs up the board, with the bishop on g5 nicely covering the king from any disturbance by the rook. Black resigned.

■ ■ ■

In his game against Teimour Radjabov on Board 2, Ian Nepomniachtchi missed a venomous tactical shot in the time-trouble phase that immediately decided the outcome of the game. As a result, Maxim Matlakov's endgame grind against Arkadij Naiditsch was just for statistics, as the match finished 3-1.

If you think that Naiditsch was in any way disheartened by this loss, you couldn't be more wrong. In Round 9, he played in incredibly inspired fashion. But let's first have a look at the standings going into the last round.

With Azerbaijan playing Ukraine, and Russia pitted against a German team that was performing very well, we were in for a treat. Russia did what they had to do and won 3-1. This meant that 2-2 would be enough for the Azeris to claim the European title, since the tie-break was in their favour. With the match tied at 1½-1½, the last game to finish was the following fascinating encounter.

**Arkadij Naiditsch
Ruslan Ponomariov**
Hersonissos 2017 (9)
Pirc Defence

1.e4 d6
The Pirc! A rare guest at top level.
2.d4 ♘f6 3.♘c3 g6 4.♗e3 c6 5.h3
There is a lot to be said about the various move-order subtleties at this point, but I guess the New In Chess Yearbook would be a more appropriate place to do that.

5...♗g7 6.♘ge2 b5 7.a3 0-0 8.g4 e5
'A flank attack should be countered in the centre!' is a well-known chess maxim, and Ponomariov's move fits right in. However, I much agree with my engine, which goes 8...a5, keeping the options in the centre open and, after for instance 9.♘g3, preparing

ChessBase

NEW!

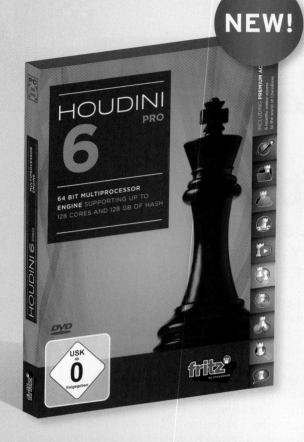

GIVE IN TO THE MAGIC!

Houdini 6

HOUDINI 6- STANDARD

The multiprocessor engine can use up to 8 cores
and 4 GB of RAM

€ 79.90

HOUDINI 6- PRO

The Pro version can run on up to 128 cores and use
128 GB of memory and is the right choice for high-
end users with powerful hardware. **€ 99.90**

Houdini 6 continues where its predecessor left off, and adds solid 60 Elo points to this formidable engine, once again making Houdini the strongest chess program currently available on the market. With Houdini 6, you not only gain in terms of computing power, but also in terms of time! The new engine delivers better performance even if you only let it calculate for half as long as the previous version!

Houdini 6 has been put to the test in various areas and thoroughly refined in all the right places: position evaluation, search, time management and use of the endgame tablebases have been improved, as has parallel processing. Houdini 6 delivers particularly exceptional results on systems with a large number of CPUs, and can run up to 128 threads on high-end hardware.

The enhanced „Tactical mode" transforms Houdini 6 into the most ingenious position solver of all time and improves again on the records held by previous versions in tactical benchmark tests. In addition, „Tactical mode" can now also be assigned an exact number of threads, giving you additional flexibility.

Despite all the detailed technical improvements, Houdini has kept its creative and imaginative style of play, and where other programs see no future or are locked into a draw, Houdini delivers surprise after surprise with hidden resources. You can certainly look forward to using this latest version of the true wizard among the chess programs!

Included in the scope of supply:

• Houdini 6 engine (Standard or Pro)
• Fritz 15 user interface
• Premium membership for playchess.com and your ChessBase Account (6 months)
• Online access to the world's largest analysis database, "Let's Check",
  with over 200 million deeply analyzed positions (6 months)

Online Shop: shop.chessbase.com · ChessBase GmbH · Osterbekstr. 90a · 22083 Hamburg · Germany · info@chessbase.com

Now with new Big / Mega Database 2018!

TRAIN LIKE CARLSEN & CO

The new ChessBase 14 program packages 2018

From "A" for analysis to "Z" for zugzwang: there are in the new ChessBase 14 program a whole heap of improvements which make the entry and analysis of games all the more easy, as they do the production of training or practice material. The new function "Assisted Analysis" is an outstanding example: as you enter a game, whenever you click on a piece an evaluation is produced for all its

possible target squares and this is highlighted on the board in colour. Thus even before you play it you can see whether there is a better move than the one you planned. This not only makes entering moves easy, but it also invites you to participate in subtle and continuous calculation training.

Also new in ChessBase 14 is the access to annotated games in the Live Database. In conjunction with a Premium Account you can even find complete analysis of many topical games from the elite tournaments. And because the Live Database has become more and more important in the search for comparable games, now as you play through a game ChessBase 14 updates the search results automatically on every move.

Other improvements: new game notation with diagrams and coloured highlighting in encapsulated variations, one login for all ChessBase servers (playchess, ChessBase Cloud, Let's Check, ChessBase Accounts), analysis of a whole game with rapid error search, saving of the search mask, export of the diagram list as a Word document produces training material in a jiffy, simplified production of training questions, replacing games in big databases considerably speeded up, improved search for doubles, easy use of tool to activate Fritz-Trainer and Engines, and much more.

Online Shop: shop.chessbase.com · ChessBase GmbH · Osterbekstr. 90a · 22083 Hamburg · Germany · info@chessbase.com

NEW FRITZ TRAINER DVDs

Yannick Pelletier:

THE HEDGEHOG - A UNIVERSAL SYSTEM AGAINST 1.c4 AND 1.Nf3

At first glance, this Black's setup might appear somewhat passive, but looks can be deceiving! Black is always waiting for a chance to take the initiative and launch a counterattack. Yannick Pelletier provides you with a complete Hedgehog repertoire against the English and the Reti. The Swiss grandmaster explains a number of theoretical variations with illustrative games.

€ 29,90

Simon Williams:

THE TACTICAL CHIGORIN

Opening with the Chigorin shows your intention to play for a win right from the outset. After 1.d4 d5 2.c4 Nc6 Black's pieces fly into the game putting pressure on White's position from a very early stage. This opening is ideal for the type of player who strives for an unconventional yet attacking game right from the start. This new DVD by Simon Williams will take you through all the things you need to know in order to play this opening in a fun and exciting way!

€ 29,90

Adrian Mikhalchishin:

PIECES, PAWNS AND SQUARES

Pieces are more difficult to handle than pawns – but sometimes they can help each other, e.g. if it's about conquering a square! But what to do once you have gained control over it? More themes covered on this DVD: how to create weaknesses, the powerful helping pawn, piece transfer to strongholds etc.

€ 29,90

Christian Bauer:

STRIKE FIRST WITH THE SCANDINAVIAN

The Scandinavian guides your opponent on much less familiar terrain than for example the Sicilian or any 1.e4 e5 system. This rareness leads to a slow evolution of theory. After 1.e4 d5 Black fights for the initiative from move one on without any precedent manoeuvring. Make the Scandinavian your opening weapon against 1.e4!

€ 29,90

Erwin l'Ami:

THE BEASTY BOTVINNIK VARIATION IN THE SEMI-SLAV

Let the Dutch grandmaster take you on a journey through what is arguably the sharpest opening line known to man: the Botvinnik Variation! Ever since its birth, in the late 30's of the previous century, the Botvinnik Variation has fascinated generations of dynamic players. To date, the opening is very much alive and is considered the sharpest and most principled way to meet 5.Bg5 in the Semi-Slav.

€ 29,90

Sergei Tiviakov:

REALIZING AN ADVANTAGE

It's a problem every player encounters when he stands better in a game: how to convert his plus into a full point? Tiviakov answers this difficult question of chess strategy, considering both the psychological aspects of the realisation of an advantage and the technical methods. Special attention is paid to the problem of piece exchanges. Recommended for players of all levels and ages!

€ 29,90

Online Shop: shop.chessbase.com · ChessBase GmbH · Osterbekstr. 90a · 22083 Hamburg · Germany · info@chessbase.com

counterplay with 9...♘a6, followed by ...b4 and ...c5.

9.d5 ♗b7 An interesting attempt to muddy the waters is 9...cxd5 10.exd5 ♘a6 11.♘xb5 ♘c7, with good play for the pawn. But much stronger is 11.♘g3 ♘c7 12.g5, when White is firmly in control.

10.♘g3 a6 One could argue that, strategically speaking, things were already becoming dangerous for Black, but this is definitely too slow. 10...a5 was a must, fighting for counterplay. When playing a dubious (statement!) opening like the Pirc, the smallest errors can lead to huge trouble.

11.g5 ♘fd7 12.h4 Stuck without counterplay and a white kingside attack about to be launched, I don't think it's an exaggeration to say that Black is lost already here. Knowing Arkadij, he probably thought exactly the same thing!

12...♖e8 13.h5 ♘b6 14.hxg6 hxg6

In the final round Arkadij Naiditsch failed to round off a great attacking game against Ruslan Ponomariov. As a draw was enough for the title, Azerbaijan's third board will not have been too upset.

15.♘f5! Classic stuff! **15...cxd5** 15...gxf5 16.exf5 ♘xd5 17.f6 is just crushing.

16.♗xb6 ♕xb6

17.♗xb5!

Fantastic! In the line 17...axb5 18.♘xg7 ♔xg7 19.♕f3 ♕d8 20.♖h7+ ♔xh7 21.♕xf7+ ♔h8 22.♔e2! it becomes clear why the bishop had to get out of the way on f1: 23.♖h1+ is coming.

17...gxf5 18.♗xe8 ♕d8 19.♕h5 ♕xe8 20.exf5 ♕e7 21.f6 ♗xf6 22.gxf6 ♕xf6 23.0-0-0 d4 From here on in, White has various faster ways to decide the game, but up until the very last moment the win is never in any doubt.

24.♘e4 ♗xe4 25.♕g4+

25...♔f8 25...♕g6 (or 25...♗g6) 26.♕c8+! forces mate on the next move.

26.♕xe4 ♖a7 27.♖d3 27.f4! would have decided the game much easier, breaking open Black's position.

27...♘d7 28.♖f3 ♕g5+ 29.♔b1 ♔e7 30.♕c6 ♘f6 31.♖h8 ♕g1+ 32.♔a2 ♕g4 33.♖h6 ♕e4 34.♕xe4 ♘xe4 35.♖xf7+ ♔xf7 36.♖h7+ ♔e6 37.♖xa7 ♘xf2 38.♔b1 e4

39.♖xa6? The horror! 39.♔c1 e3, and now 40.b4!, was the prophylactic measure that needed to be taken in order to win the game. Now 40...d3 41.cxd3 ♘xd3+ 42.♔d1 wins in straightfor-

Hersonissos open 2017

		MP	BP
1	Azerbaijan	14	25
2	Russia	14	22
3	Ukraine	13	23
4	Croatia	13	18½
5	Hungary	12	22½
6	Israel	12	20
7	Romania	12	20½
8	Germany	11	21
9	Netherlands	11	20
10	Poland	11	20½
11	Turkey	11	19½
12	Armenia	10	19
13	Spain	10	19½
14	Czech Republic	10	19
15	Italy	10	16½
16	England	10	18
17	Slovakia	10	18
18	Belarus	9	20
19	Georgia	9	19
20	France	9	18½
21	Slovenia	9	19½
22	Serbia	9	20½
23	Norway	9	18½
24	Austria	9	15½
25	Greece 1	8	20
26	Greece 2	8	17
27	Iceland	8	18
28	FYROM	8	18½
29	Moldova	8	17
30	Switzerland	8	18
31	Finland	7	14
32	Montenegro	7	16½
	40 teams 9 rounds		

us a rare insight in how tensions can rise in Russian chess circles when team events are the topic. Only moments after Sergey Karjakin had tweeted his congratulations to the Russian women's team (more about that further on) and in that same tweet had acknowledged that in the Open section the Russian team had fought well till the end but lacked a little something, Ian Nepomniachtchi asked Karjakin whether he would like to teach them how to feel like a winner despite not having won – a direct reference to his World Championship match in New York last year. Sergey initially reacted calmly, coolly pointing out that he would do so the moment 'Nepo' would play such a match. From here on in, the conversation took a remarkably unpleasant turn, and it was only the next day that the two settled their differences publicly as well.

Am I really not going to mention my own team, the Netherlands? Unfortunately, we couldn't compete for medals this time, but our last board, Jorden van Foreest, did take bronze on Board 5! That was not the only way in which he stole the limelight.

Jorden van Foreest
Jure Skoberne
Hersonissos 2017 (9)

position after 53...♖c2+

Here Jorden felt that 54.♞xg2 ♖xg2 55.♖xe3 should be winning and duly took the bishop off the board. His opponent immediately stopped the clock and for a moment, Jorden thought the point was in the pocket. After it was pointed out to him that his king was in check, the diagrammed position was restored and two minutes were deducted from his clock. Jorden now went **54.♔b6**, and after a few more adventures – but no further illegal moves – he won the game on move 69.

ward fashion. One can immediately see the difference with the game:
39...e3 40.♔c1
40.♖a8 ♔e7 41.♔c1 d3 42.cxd3 ♞xd3+ 43.♔d1 ♞xb2+ 44.♔e2 ♞c4 45.♖a7+ ♔e6 46.a4 was surely a better try, but 46...♔d5 47.♔d3 ♔e6!? holds. If White pushes 48.a5 then 48...♞e5+ 49.♔xe3 ♞c6 50.♖a8 ♔d7 51.♔e4 ♔c7 52.♔d5 ♔b7 wins the a-pawn, securing the draw.
40...d3 41.cxd3 ♞xd3+ 42.♔d1 ♞xb2+ 43.♔e2 ♞c4 And draw agreed, which meant first place for the Azeris.

The 2-2 tie also meant that Ukraine secured bronze, and while the Azeris started their celebrations, Twitter gave

Jorden van Foreest and Dutch team captain Loek van Wely. Van Foreest won a bronze medal on Board 5, but had to work a bit longer than expected in his game against Jure Skoberne.

MARIA EMELIANOVA

Russian women win again

In the Women's section, there was simply no stopping the pre-tournament favourites from Russia. The biggest match-up, between Russia and Georgia, took place in Round 4 and was won by Russia (2½-1½). It was Kateryna Lagno (gold medal on Board 2) who scored an important point against Nino Batsiashvili.

Kateryna Lagno
Nino Batsiashvili
Hersonissos 2017 (4)

position after 23.♘c6

23...♖xe1+ 24.♔xe1 ♖xd1+ 25.♔xd1 ♘c8 looks a bit awkward, but once you see ♔e8-d7 is coming, expelling the knight, you realize the position is a pretty straightforward draw. In the game, following **23...♖xd1?! 24.♖xd1 a6**

25.♖d6!, Black was in a nasty bind. Batsiashvili eventually succumbed in the rook ending after **25...♖c8**

The successful Russian women and their trainers: Alexander Riazantsev, Evgeny Najer, Olga Girya, Sergey Rublevsky, Alexandra Kosteniuk, Aleksandra Goryachkina and Valentina Gunina.

26.♘e5 f6 27.♖xb6 fxe5 28.♖xa6 (1-0, 51)

Another big match-up was seen on Board 3. In the diagrammed position, Valentina Gunina had just pushed 35...g6-g5.

Bela Khotenashvili
Valentina Gunina
Hersonissos 2017 (4)

position after 35...g5

White is under considerable pressure, but the remarkable 36.♘g1!! would most likely have held the balance. Now 36....gxh4 37.♗h2, followed by ♔h1, ♖bb2 is far from clear. In the game followed: **36.♕d2 gxh4**

37.♗h2

37...h3+! and next saw Gunina undermine the f3-pawn and then obtain a winning advantage that she converted without difficulty.

The fact that Georgia's Leva Javakishvili defeated Olga Girya on last board couldn't stop Russia from winning the match, as Alexandra Kosteniuk made a solid draw on Board 1. With the three top boards scoring 18½ out of 24 games and the team only dropping one match point, against Poland, it is no wonder the Russian ladies had already secured first place with one round to spare. In that 8th round, Russia defeated Turkey 4-0.

Former World Champion Alexandra Kosteniuk, who took gold on the first board (6 from 8, a 2632 performance) was the team's strong and confident leader.

NOTES BY
Alexandra Kosteniuk

Ekaterina Atalik
Alexandra Kosteniuk
Hersonissos 2017 (8)
Bogo-Indian Defence

The victory in the European Team championship was already the 5th European gold for the Russian women. The first gold medals were won exactly 10 years ago at the exact

9.d5?
After the game, my teammate Ekaterina Lagno was wondering, 'How could White even think about playing d5 with the knight on d2?' I like this short remark, which explains where White's problems in this game originated from. Usually White keeps the tension in the centre and opts for 9.b4, 9.♕c2 or 9.♖e1.

'Who could have imagined 25 years ago that we'd still be playing chess against each other in 2017 ☺ '

same place, and I was also leading the Russian women's team at that time. That was not the only 'deja-vu' for me during this event. I can't avoid my childhood memories when I meet over the board with some of the girls I started playing against so long ago. My first game with Ekaterina Atalik – then still called Ekaterina Polovnikova – was played in 1992 in my first ever Russian girls' championship in Lipetsk. Since Ekaterina is two years older than me it was a difficult encounter. Who could have imagined 25 years ago that we'd still be playing chess against each other in 2017? ☺

1.d4 ♘f6 2.c4 e6 3.♘f3 ♗b4+
The preparation for the game sometimes takes as much time as the game itself, but it is such a good feeling when this preparation pays off.
4.♘bd2 0-0 5.a3 ♗e7 6.e4 d6 7.♗e2 ♘bd7 8.0-0 e5

9...a5
With the idea of playing ...a4 and also to secure the c5-square for my knight. Still, starting with ...♘c5 seems to be more precise.
10.b3 ♘c5 11.♕c2 ♘h5!

It's usually a promising sign when short tactics start to favour one side. This move is possible since 12.♘xe5 won't work now in view of the intermediate move 12...♘f4!.

12.g3

One of a few crossroads in this game for me. I spent some time trying to figure out if I needed to play ...♗h3 and then ...f5, or whether it would be better to keep the bishop on c8 and play ...f5 at once. I decided that including the moves 12...♗h3 13.♖e1 would favour me, since with the white rook on e1, the lines after 14.♘xe5 look better for me.

12...♗h3
In case of 12...f5 13.♘xe5, the black pawn on f5 would be hanging after 13...♘xg3 14.fxg3 dxe5 because of White's rook on the f-file. Instead of 13...♘xg3, I can play 13...♘f6, but it doesn't yield Black more than equality after 14.♘d3 ♘fxe4 15.♗b2 (15.f3? is bad because of 15...♗f6; but 15.♖b1!? might be interesting, with the idea of developing the bishop to e3).

13.♖e1 f5

During the game I wasn't sure whether I needed to play ...f5 immediately, thus allowing White to play ♘xe5 (and I wasn't that sure that the ensuing complications would give me an advantage), or whether I could just protect my knight on h5 by playing 13...g6, preparing ...f5 for the next moves. But in the end, after some calculations, I decided to go for the straightforward move.

14.♗b2?

This move gives Black more time to consolidate and bring more pieces to the kingside. The critical capture on e5 was the only option for White to stay in the game:

14.♘xe5! ♘xg3 (now 14...♘f6 is not a good option for Black because of 15.♘d3) 15.hxg3 (15.fxg3 doesn't work without the rook on f1, since the f-file and the white king's position become too exposed to the invading black pieces: 15...dxe5 16.♗b2 ♗g5 17.♗xe5 ♗e3+ 18.♔h1 ♕e7) 15...dxe5 16.♔h2

and now:

A) 16...f4 might seem like a good try, but unfortunately for Black, White has some defensive resources: 17.♔xh3 fxg3 18.f4! The only move, but can you name me a player who would be able to make it? Other options give Black a crucial attack. I particularly enjoyed Black's rook manoeuvre in the following line: 18.f3 g2 19.♔xg2 ♖a6! (I simply love this rook transfer) 20.♖h1 ♖g6+ 21.♔f1 ♗h4 and White's pieces are not coordinated enough to resist against Black's pressure.

B) Probably better is 16...♗g4, when after 17.f3 f4 18.fxg4 fxg3+, 19.♔h3! is the only move for White, and I failed to find a win for Black. Still, during a practical game it should be nearly impossible for a human being not to get checkmated.

14...♕e8

On Boards 1 and 2, Alexandra Kosteniuk (6/8) and Kateryna Lagno (6½/8) showed the Russian women the way to another European title.

The knight on h5 is protected now and it's getting difficult for White to play.

15.b4?

This almost loses the game, White had to take on f5. Of course her position is worse, but at least there is no direct way for Black to turn this advantage into a full point yet.

15...♘xe4 16.♘xe4 fxe4 17.♘d2

Another crossroads. I spent almost 20 minutes here, trying to find the most precise way to proceed.

After 17.♕xe4 I was planning to play 17...♘f4! 18.♗f1 (18.gxf4 ♖xf4 19.♕c2 ♖g4+ winning) 18...♕h5. and White is struggling.

17...axb4

Instead, 17...e3! would have been more accurate, but I thought that the exchange on b4, and then on a1, couldn't be a bad idea in this position. Unfortunately, after 17...axb4 White is given time to consolidate at the cost of a pawn, which was the lesser evil. Another interesting move that I was thinking about was 17...♘f4!?, but it didn't appeal to me as much as the lines with ...e3, although Black is still better after 18.♘xe4 ♕g6, and it's not so easy for White to play, since her king is not feeling secure.

18.axb4

Probably the last mistake.

Trying to eliminate the knight didn't
work for White: 18.♗xh5 ♕xh5
19.axb4 ♖xa1 20.♗xa1 ♗g5!, the
favourite place for the dark-squared
bishop in this position, and Black is
winning. But it was a good moment
to give a pawn with 18.♘xe4!?, hoping
to hang on.

18...♖xa1 19.♗xa1
19.♖xa1 doesn't change a lot: 19...e3
20.fxe3 ♗g5.
**19...e3 20.fxe3 ♗g5! 21.♕d3
♘f6!**
Not letting White's knight come to
e4: 21...♕f7 22.♘e4.
22.♗f3

This position is hopeless for White,
Black has several ways to win, while
White doesn't have any counterchances at all.
22.♗b2 runs into 22...♕g6!, and
22.♘e4 ♘xe4 23.♕xe4 loses to
23...♕f7.
22...♕f7 23.♕e2 ♘g4

Strong moves in such positions are
usually not very difficult to find.
24.♗xg4 ♗xg4 25.♕g2 ♗h3!
Another simple yet very strong move.
26.♕e2 ♕g6 27.♖c1

27...h5 My target was the white king.
The computer suggests ...♖a8-a2
as an option, but I didn't even look
in that direction. **28.♔h1 ♗g4
29.♕e1 ♕h6 30.♖c3 h4 31.♔g1**

31...♗h3 During the game I didn't
realize how good my position was
after 31...hxg3 32.♕xg3 (32.hxg3
♕h3 33.♖a3 ♖f6! and on to h6, with
checkmate coming soon) 32...♕h5.
But the text-move, 31...♗h3, was not
so bad either.
32.♗b2 ♕h5 33.♗c1 ♕g4

It's difficult to believe, but Black's
queen doesn't belong here. The
main winning ideas in this position
are connected with opening up the
h-file and bringing the rook to h6 via
f6. During the game I was trying to

Once again the Creta Maris Beach Resort in Hersonissos was a comfortable venue for a major chess event.

and creates considerable technical difficulties.

45.♗c5! It's important to block the rook's exit, although at this point it's hard to see why.

45...♔f6 46.♔f4 As 46.♔e3 ♔e5! would lose the e4-pawn.

46...♗g7

How to proceed? After all, 47...♗h6+ is a serious threat.

47.g5+! ♔g6 48.♔e3! ♔xg5 49.a4!, and here it all becomes clear. The black king has been lured away from e5, and now 49...♔f6 50.♔d3 ♔e5 51.a5 ♖xe4 52.a6 is just winning, while if 49...bxa4, 50.♔d3 rounds up the rook. Very pretty! Black resorted to **49...♗d4+ 50.♗xd4 ♖xb4,** but had to resign soon. ∎

make the idea of ...♖f3 work, but it is not enough to break through.

34.b5 b6

A move you simply can't resist, especially if you're moving closer to the time-control.

35.♔h1

This loses on the spot. But White is almost in zugzwang; she can only move her rook along the third rank, while all other moves are losing.

After 35.♖a3 I would have needed to find the right set-up by playing 35...♕h5 and going for the plan with the h-file attack. And I should mention that 35.♗b2 allows 35...♖f3!.

35...♖f1+! Yet again, not a very difficult move to find, but such a pleasant one to play ☺.

36.♕xf1 ♗xf1 37.♘xf1 ♕e2

White resigned.

∎ ∎ ∎

Besides experienced trainer Elizbar Ubilava, the Georgian team had also brought along a surprise 'assistant coach', Indian grandmaster Adhiban Baskaran. From what I could observe from a distance, I think the mix of experience and youth worked wonders, since the Georgians deservedly took silver.

Let me finish with a fragment from Bela Khotenashvili's last-round win against Italy. Bela won gold on Board 3, and I liked how she wrapped up this game.

**Bela Khotenashvili
Desiree Di Benedetto**
Hersonissos 2017 (9)

position after 44...fxe6

White is a pawn up, but the black pawn on c3 is a strong passed pawn

	Hersonissos women 2017	MP	BP
1	Russia	16	25½
2	Georgia	14	25½
3	Ukraine	13	23
4	Poland	12	20½
5	Romania	12	21
6	Spain	11	21
7	Israel	11	22
8	Azerbaijan	11	19½
9	Armenia	11	18
10	Italy	10	19½
11	Greece 1	10	19
12	Hungary	10	19
13	Turkey	10	15½
14	Netherlands	9	18½
15	Serbia	9	18
16	Germany	9	19½
17	Lithuania	9	20
18	Switzerland	9	16
19	Austria	9	16½
20	Belarus	8	18½
21	Czech Republic	8	20
22	France	8	16½
23	FYROM	8	15½
24	Slovenia	7	19
25	Croatia	7	17½
26	England	7	14½
27	Slovakia	7	18½
28	Norway	7	13½
29	Belgium	6	13½
30	Greece 2	4	13
31	Finland	3	8½
32	Montenegro	2	10
	32 teams 9 rounds		

Is Blitz a drug?

Or a fun playground where a lot can be learned?

THEY SAY THAT HE HADN'T PLAYED BLITZ FOR SIX DAYS!

BLITZ IS BLISS

Brotherhood OF THE QUICK FIX

BEREND VONK

It's so good that sometimes we wished it didn't exist. Who hasn't played blitz for hours and hours and wondered: Am I an addict? Is this a drug? **JENNIFER VALLENS** takes a look at the dark and bright sides of speed chess and explains how getting your fix may fix your game.

Bam! The slam of the clock, pieces are flying everywhere, hands flailing as one hand moves a piece while the other hand stands up pieces that have been knocked off the board. You are left with seconds on the clock, your heart is pumping out of your chest, your foot is furiously tapping. You are down a piece, you have a losing position *and* your king is exposed! But, then, in grease lightning speed, you see a way to sac your queen and throw your opponent off guard. He hesitates... and he flags! He lost on time, another one bites the dust! But there is little respite. In an automatic gesture the pieces are being put in the their starting positions again, the clock is reset. The only follow-up for a blitz game is... another one!

Intoxicating

You don't often put the words fast, noise and mess together when you are discussing chess. But speed chess is a different animal altogether. In blitz, as speed chess is commonly called, the drama of an entire game – or even more – is compressed in a time span of literally minutes. There are more mistakes and blunders and many classic chess rules are thrown out of the window. Small wonder, as in the most popular time rates you only have 3 or 5 minutes for the entire game. Or slightly more if you play with increments of a couple of seconds per move. Or even far less, if you play bullet, which allows you only one minute for a game.

The pounding of the clock and the mess of the pieces on the board is often combined with boisterous trash talk that charges the air and often draws attention from a crowd. The energy of the crowd, the thrill of the moment, the fear of flagging and the potential of dramatically crushing your opponent, can be intoxicating.

Playing blitz can certainly bring up the same feelings one might associate with methamphetamine, commonly known as speed. This isn't a coincidence. When you are racing the clock playing a game of blitz or bullet, your heart rate starts to increase, your palms get sweaty and as the adrenaline pumps throughout your body, the feel-good chemical dopamine is being released, causing you to feel, for lack of another word, high.

Insanity, passion and addiction
Playing in front of a crowd may be the ideal setting for the excitement that blitz can create, but – as most of us know only too well – many more people play speed chess in the confines of their own home, behind a computer screen. The flying of the pieces may not be present and the cheering of the crowd is lost, but the adrenaline rush remains. And some believe it might be more addictive to play blitz online.

As English GM Danny Gormally, the author of **Insanity, Passion and Addiction: A year inside the chess world**, a book dedicated to his chess addiction, wrote to us: 'Having speed chess available 24 hours a day, 7 days a week only adds to the temptation to play "just one more game". The problem is that while a chess club that exists in the real world will have to close at some point, online chess never closes.'

US chess blogger and chess coach,

Michael Aigner, opines: 'Speed chess hooks a player just like a good video game. When you lose, the natural temptation is to press the "Play Again" button and start over.'

And conservative columnist and political commentator Charles Krauthammer said about chess: 'It's like alcohol. It's a drug. I have to control it, or it could overwhelm me.' He felt the danger more acutely than ever when he started playing on the Internet Chess Club. In an article in *Time Magazine* in 2000, he famously described the ICC as 'It's so satisfying it should be illegal.'

These days the ICC is one of many online websites where chess players can get their fix 24/7. Chess.com, Chess24, Playchess and Lichess are just as popular or even bigger, and there are many more.

But they all create a permanent blitz environment that for many users is too good to be true. Mike

Klein, Director of Content for Chess. com, recalls having a member write to him asking him to lock him out of his account because he couldn't control himself to stop playing on his own.

The ICC reports that the most played speed chess games on their site of all time by one user is over 640,000 games. The most bullet games played on their site is by a WFM who goes by the user name lollipop and has played a total of 327,645 games.

Popular time-controls

Chess.com gets between 8,000 and 10,000 new members a day. The number of games that are being played is staggering. A total of more than 2 billion games have been played since 2007, a memorable mark that was passed this summer. Not surprisingly, the faster time-controls prove the most attractive. Here is a list of the most popular time-controls and the number of games played with them over a recent period of 24 hours. (10/0 means, ten minutes per game per player, no increment; 5/5 means five minutes per game per player, with a 5 second increment per move).

10/0	498,000		
5/0	377,000	2/1	63,000
3/0	335,000	15/10	50,000
1/0	282,000	5/5	50,000
3/2	71,000	30/0	46,000

> 'The ICC reports that the most played speed chess games on their site of all time by one user is over 640,000 games.'

On Chess.com, launched 12 years after the ICC was founded, the most active user goes by the name of Peace-MyFriend. He or she has been a member from 2007 and so far has played 262,207 blitz games. The most active titled player on Chess.com is gmjoey1 (Rogelio Antonio from the Philippines) with 97,213 bullet and 32,685 blitz games. Is this too much? What is too much?

Instant gratifying reward
The American Psychiatric Association (APA) added Internet Gaming Addiction as one of the potential disorders that need to be treated. The APA explains that Internet gaming activates reward systems similarly to using drugs. The euphoric feeling when you win a match or unlock an achievement is the same as getting high, as both activities trigger dopamine releases in the brain. When addicts get engrossed playing

online games, certain pathways in their brains are triggered in the same direct and intense way that a drug addict's brain is affected by a particular substance.

There are even hospitals across America, China and Korea which help people suffering from gaming addiction. Statistics show that 10% of all 30 million gamers in China are addicted to online gaming. For the US, data from the American Medical Association shows that 15% of all gamers, or approximately five million people, are addicted.

The allure of speed chess then isn't about playing the best move. It isn't about the beauty of the position,

> **Nakamura states 'Blitz is just getting positions where you can move fast. I mean it's not chess.'**

the brilliant attack or the depth of calculation. It's a cheap thrill, a shot of adrenaline, an instant gratifying reward.

The effects of an adrenaline rush increase manifold. The more you play, the more you get. Because bullet chess is played with one minute on the clock, you are getting a spike in dopamine every minute, opposed to blitz, which could be every 10 minutes. The problem is that you start to build up a tolerance to it and you need to play more to get the same high.

English IM and commentator Lawrence Trent acknowledged: 'When I play speed chess I definitely experience a rush. It's a testosterone booster for sure. I really, really enjoy playing bullet chess online. I have

played tens of thousands of games and still get the urge to play, a lot. Though I've calmed down compared to a few years ago, bullet, for me, is the ultimate thrill. I still get a kick out of flagging someone in a lost position, or saving a game when I am busted, or even just playing a great attacking game in such a short period of time'.

WGM Jennifer Shahade, who is also a poker player, commentator and author, looks at it from a broader perspective: 'The rush of seeing your rating go up or down online may make online blitz even more addictive, but I also think that over-the-board blitz and bullet is addictive. It's fun and tactile, and late night blitz and bullet sessions are actually an important staple of improving a player's diet. It keeps chess fun and leads to lifelong friendships.'

And, of course, the fastness of it all already provides a kick in itself. In 2013, Hikaru Nakamura and Bruce Harper released a book on the fastest form of speed chess, *Bullet Chess: One Minute to Mate*. The first line of the first chapter of their book is: 'Experienced players will likely spend less than a minute on this chapter, but that's the whole idea of bullet chess, isn't it?'

Detrimental effects

The issue of addiction is one potential threat of playing a lot of speed chess. But the question of whether playing a lot of speed chess can damage one's slow game, is also a matter of concern for many. One of the fiercest critics of the detrimental effects of blitz was Mikhail Botvinnik (1911-1995) and one gets the impression that the oft repeated condemnation of fast games by the father of Soviet Chess had a huge impact. Even in the last decades of the 20th century official blitz competitions among the chess elite were a rarity.

Many chess purists did not or do not consider speed chess as chess, but merely as a variation of the game. While classic chess is about deep

The World of Chess

With 188 member federations, FIDE is one of the biggest sports organizations in the world. The global strength of chess can be gleaned from the following figures that Chess.com provided: the number of players from the most active countries that played on their website over a recent period of 24 hours. The second figure indicates how many of them were titled players.

1.	United States	304,066	701
2.	India	90,928	43
3.	United Kingdom	46,796	38
4.	Russia	43,738	137
5.	Canada	37,895	72
6.	Norway	25,628	32
7.	Spain	25,434	56
8.	Mexico	24,272	15
9.	Germany	24,115	80
10.	Philippines	23,432	30
11.	France	23,181	68
12.	Australia	22,442	44
13.	Brazil	22,124	59
14.	Turkey	21,720	23
15.	Italy	21,086	38
16.	Netherlands	20,857	68
17.	Indonesia	14,998	13
18.	Argentina	13,930	27
19.	Ukraine	13,009	73

strategies and out-thinking your opponent, speed chess is mainly about time and the pressure that is created when you have so little of it. People play because the rush of crushing an opponent under ruthless conditions is exciting, as well as the unpredictable outcome that keeps one on the edge of their seat. And they get, perhaps unexpected, support from the blitz maverick himself, Nakamura, who states 'Blitz is just getting positions where you can move fast. I mean it's not chess.'

Raising the stakes

Playing blitz for money adds to the excitement of the game. While Nakamura commented that he thinks blitz is without question addictive, he added with a smirk, 'and when you raise the stakes and play for money, it only becomes more fun.'

Asa Hoffmann, a New York FM and chess teacher, who features in the movie *Searching for Bobby Fischer*, made a living off playing blitz games in the 1960s, $5 at a time. Now 74, Hoffmann told us that his longtime friend Bobby Fischer 'would only play blitz for money and would play for odds 10-1 or in some cases 20-1 and he hardly ever lost a game.' He remembers how he once played Bobby at the Henry Hudson Hotel in New York, a 20-1 odds blitz game. Hoffmann unexpectedly won the first battle that day throwing Fischer off with the Evans Gambit, shocking all that watched, including Bobby himself. 'Bobby annoyingly fished out $1 bills out of his pockets to pay up. Bobby wanted to play again, but he no longer had even a dollar to ante up. We all staked him so that we all could play Bobby more games. We continued to play, with Bobby winning most, if not all the games after that.'

Fischer once remarked that 'Blitz chess kills your ideas', but just like most great champions he was a formidable blitz player. His win at the Herceg Novi blitz tournament in 1970, where he scored an unbelievable 19/22 against the world's best and finished 4½ points ahead of Mikhail Tal, remains one of the most legendary blitz feats of all time. And it wasn't only about being quicker than his opponents. According to Tal, his American rival barely made any mistakes.

Rook odds

For our current World Champion, Magnus Carlsen, blitz can be both an awful lot of fun and a very serious matter. The fun part was manifest in one of the most stunning bets in modern chess. At the end of the 2015 Sinquefield Cup, as the players and other guests were relaxing at the St. Louis Chess Club, Carlsen played a blitz match with the already mentioned Lawrence Trent, offering the English IM rook(!) odds in 3-minute blitz. Carlsen bet Trent he would score 4 points from 10 games. Trent couldn't believe it – and who

could blame him? – and eagerly accepted the challenge. But after 9 games, Carlsen, starting with a rook down, had already scored 4 points! Indeed, the crowd at the club went crazy. How special this feat was, was proven by Maxime Vachier-Lagrave, who immediately offered Trent the same bet and lost all 10 games.

How seriously Magnus Carlsen takes blitz chess was once again shown in his Champions Showdown match against Chinese number one Ding Liren, that is reported on elsewhere in this issue. And his fanaticism has been seen numerous other times when the Norwegian took part in major blitz championships. It wasn't for nothing that he was one of the first to sign up for the upcoming Rapid & Blitz World Championships in Riyadh.

Training tool

Many prominent players believe that blitz is not only great fun, but also an adequate and useful training tool. One of them is Sergey Karjakin, Carlsen's challenger in the 2016 World Championship match and the current Blitz World Champion. The Russian grandmaster says that he doesn't play a lot of blitz, but that when he does, he takes it very seriously. He affirms that when he was younger, playing blitz online was certainly fun, but also useful. 'Back then you could play experienced, strong players like Alexander Grischuk, who may play you blitz, but might not be willing to put in the time for a classical game.'

Alexander Grischuk has won the Blitz World Championship three times. After his third victory in Berlin in 2015, he told Chess.com that he is better at playing blitz games than slower-paced contests. And if it was up to him the faster chess disciplines would be much more important, perhaps he wouldn't even mind if classical chess was abolished.

The current number 2 in the overall world rankings certainly

THE MAN WHO PLAYED 640.000 BLITZGAMES ON ICC

...IT'S MY DAY OFF...

...70 GAMES MAX...

BEREND VONK

VONK

doesn't want to go that far, but Levon Aronian also insists that blitz can be useful if you take it seriously. He himself plays blitz to keep in shape. As in his case it can be difficult to find a player of similar strength, he usually arranges set matches against strong colleagues online.

The use of blitz as a training tool is echoed by many others. Judit Polgar, Hungarian Grandmaster and arguably the strongest female chess player of all time, said in a Perpetual Chess podcast interview that she played tens of thousands of blitz games when she was little as part of her training. She further commented without question that if she was starting out today, she would be playing lots of online blitz on a daily basis.

GM Maurice Ashley remembers back in the day playing blitz for 12-14 hours non-stop on a Friday night till the sun came up. He and his friends would also play Friday-Sunday, stopping only for naps and food (and the occasional shower). His opinion is that to play well over 100 games in one sitting can be a test of one's mental toughness.

The boons of blitz

One of the biggest advocates of blitz, both as a passion and a way to get better at chess in general, is Maxim Dlugy, the former number 1 of the now defunct World Blitz Association, originally founded by the late Walter Browne, a lifelong promotor of blitz. The 1985 Junior World Champion thanks playing blitz for his being good at chess. In his 2017 book *Grandmasters Insides*, he even devotes a whole chapter to the pros of using blitz as a preparation tool for chess improvement. According to Dlugy, here are just a few key benefits of how playing blitz actually helps your chess play:

- Blitz helps you learn to make decisions faster
- Blitz lets you try out new openings

and ideas without being afraid of the result
- Blitz allows you to practice lots of chess without going to serious tournaments.

Another benefit of playing blitz as part of your training program is that it allows you to work on time control. NM Dan Heisman, author of eight chess books, advises that when you play speed games, you should use the same increment or time delay as your important games. He insists that this trains your brain how much leeway you have each move when your time runs short.

When to quit

Speed chess, however, is not for the weak. Frustration and anxiety abound. Blunders and mouse slips happen frequently. Time forfeitures in winning positions are frequent as well. Depth of calculation is compromised. Blitz encourages unsound risk taking. You entice mistakes in others and reinforce bad habits when you are playing quickly for traps. These strategies work well in fast games, but can be detrimental if you rely on them for slow games.

But good or bad, knowing when to quit is paramount. There is no question that being addicted to blitz is not nearly as destructive as, say, being addicted to gambling, smoking or even extreme sports. The chances of you losing your house, getting arrested, injured or jeopardizing your health from playing blitz are unlikely. But if you find that you start to neglect your hygiene and forget to shower or if you are constantly calling in sick to work, begin to lie to your spouse, or, heaven forbid, develop bad habits that affect your slow game, then it might be time to call in the professionals!

Bottom line is, too much of anything is bad. It is all about moderation. Some players find they can stop with little temptation to continue. Others have to take extreme measures to quit. If you are simply trying to recoup lost

rating points, much like a poker player on tilt, then you probably need to stop. Nakamura voiced 'if you're winning a lot of games on the board *and* the clock, you know you're on form. But if your wins are primarily on time in a lost position, then it might be time to quit and preserve your rating before the tide turns against you.'

Excessive and addicted

But really, isn't having a dependence or being addicted to something only considered bad, unhealthy or problematic when it interferes with your daily living? Many people describe their marathon sessions playing blitz as a state of flow. A study was conducted in 2010 and concluded there was a difference between an excessive gamer and an addicted gamer. They had two players who spent an equal amount of time 14 hours a day gaming. The difference was the motivation, experience and meaning in gaming. The addicted gamer experienced withdrawal once he was away from the game. Over time, he had developed dependence to gaming, creating conflict with his life. The excessive gamer didn't experience any withdrawal. He did not neglect responsibilities and even met his girlfriend through online games.

The study supports the argument that Internet Gaming addiction, and in my opinion, blitz, can be similar to drug addiction, but only to the extent of the symptoms such as withdrawal, mood changes or negligence. If the rush of playing speed chess becomes a compulsion and interferes with your daily life, causing you to no longer enjoy playing, then by all means, quit. But losing track of time and being able to spend hours doing something that brings you intense joy and may even improve your chess game, how bad can that be?

Anything can be addictive if you are predisposed to it. If you have an addictive or obsessive personality and speed chess provides your fix, then the good news is, at least it won't kill you. ∎

Aryan Tari
Junior World Champion

First Norwegian in history to win the title

Going into the last round with a half point lead, 18-year-old Aryan Tari successfully defended a difficult position – as Magnus Carlsen tweeted 'the mark of a champion' – to win the Junior World Championship in Tarvisio, Italy. The Norwegian took the title on tiebreak, ahead of Manuel Petrosyan (Armenia) and Aravindh Chithambaran (India). Amid celebrations on his return home Tari annotated his key win against Grigoriy Oparin, one of the pre-tournament favourites.

Another Norwegian world champion arrives at Oslo Airport.

NOTES BY ARYAN TARI

Grigoriy Oparin
Aryan Tari
Tarvisio 2017 (8)
Caro-Kann, Advance Variation

1.e4 c6 2.d4 d5 3.e5 ♗f5 4.g4
This was played instantly by Oparin. I hadn't looked at this line for a long time, and must admit I got a bit nervous when he played it.

4...♗g6
4...♗e4! seems to be more precise. Provoking f3 helps Black: 5.f3 ♗g6 6.e6 (6.h4 h5 7.e6 ♕d6 8.exf7+ ♔xf7 9.♗e3 hxg4 10.fxg4 ♘f6 11.♘c3 ♕e6 12.♗d2 ♘xg4 was the game Vallejo-So from the recent World Cup in Tbilisi, where White didn't have much fun...) 6...fxe6 7.h4 h5 8.♗d3 ♗xd3 9.♕xd3 ♕d6 10.♘e2 ♘d7, and Black is ready to play ...e5 and should be completely fine.

Nepomniachtchi-Anand, Leuven 2017, saw 4...♗d7 5.♘c3 e6 6.♗e3 ♘e7 7.♕d2 h5 8.gxh5 ♘f5 9.0-0-0, and this game ended in a draw after 41 moves. I'm not a fan of this for Black.

5.e6 ♕d6
I was basically out of book and thinking on every move.
After 5...fxe6 White can choose between 6.♘f3 and 6.h4.

6.exf7+ ♗xf7 7.f4

7...♘f6

Here, 7...g5! was a nice move, sacrificing a pawn to fight in the centre: 8.fxg5 ♘d7 9.♘f3 h5, with counterplay for Black.

8.♘c3 ♘bd7 9.♗h3

Oparin was blitzing out his moves up to this point, and it always feels uncomfortable when your opponent is playing fast. I spent about 25 minutes here, and decided that my next move was a solid practical one.

9...g5!?

Now at least I was very happy that my opponent had started thinking. I wasn't sure about my g5 push, but it looked fun, since things will get messy and it will be equally hard for him to calculate.

9...g6 looked like the logical move: 10.♘f3 ♗g7 (10...♕e6+ 11.♘e2 hands White the initiative; 10...♘e4!? is what the computer thinks is interesting: 11.♘xe4 dxe4 12.♘e5 ♗e6, and Stockfish thinks Black is fine, but this doesn't seem natural to a human with the pawn on e4) 11.0-0 0-0 12.♗e3, but playing natural moves just doesn't work and this is a depressing position for Black, since he is very passive.

First Norwegian

One of the reasons why Aryan Tari is the first Norwegian Junior World Champion is the fact that Magnus Carlsen was simply too strong to bother to play for the title. The best result so far was Simen Agdestein's second place (on tiebreak) in 1986 behind Chile's Walter Arencibia (but ahead of a.o. Vishy Anand). With his performance in Italy, Tari – the son of Iranian parents who emigrated to Norway before he was born – overtook Agdestein on the rating list and is now Norway's third player, with a 2593 rating, behind Carlsen (2837) and Jon Ludvig Hammer (2620).

10.fxg5 ♘e4

11.♘ge2

Here 11.♘xe4 was the critical line, when after 11...dxe4 12.♘e2 0-0-0 13.♗g2 the position is hard to assess. It remains messy and double-edged, I would say.

11...♗g7?!

Since Black prefers to avoid the knight swap on e4, it would have made more sense to exchange on c3: 11...♘xc3 12.bxc3 h6!?.

12.0-0?!

Better was 12.♘xe4 dxe4 13.c3!. The big problem for Black is the f5-square, which this variation shows: 13...e5 (13...0-0 14.♘g3 ♗c4, and I thought I should have compensation here when I played 8...g5, but the knight lands on f5 and kills everything) 14.♘g3, and with the knight coming to f5, White has a clear advantage.

12...0-0?!

Missing the opportunity to play 12...h6!.

13.♗e3

Again, 13.♘xe4 dxe4 14.c3! should

have been played, when after 14...♗c4 15.♗e3 e5 16.♖xf8+ ♖xf8 17.♘g3 White has the better chances.

13...♕b6!

This seemed to be the only move to create anything.

After 13...♘xc3 14.bxc3 e5 15.♘g3! was again the problem.

14.♗f4?

This came as a total surprise, and I cannot understand this move. The bishop is misplaced on f4, but I guess Oparin must have missed my next move.

The most logical move was 14.b3, and I couldn't understand why Oparin didn't go for it. I thought White might be better after 14...♘xc3 15.♘xc3 e5 16.♘e2!. An annoying move, again looking at f5, and I remember I was afraid of him going for this.

14...♘xc3!

Now Black gets ...e5 with tempo.

15.bxc3 e5

Suddenly everything has changed, and it is clear that Black will be in time with everything, besides having huge compensation for the pawn, of course.

16.♗g3?!

Taking the square away from the knight. Now I was sure that I had a fantastic position.

I wasn't quite sure about 16.♗c1, but after 16...♗g6 17.♘g3 ♖xf1+ 18.♗xf1 ♕e6 Black is just too active, and the f5-square doesn't help White that much anymore. White's best would be 19.♕e2, since he still has at least a strong knight on g3. Bad is 19.♗h3 exd4 20.cxd4 ♗xc2!.

16...♘c4

Now Black is in charge. In a practical game, it is extremely hard to try and fight in such positions. Still, it went down surprisingly fast for White.

17.♖f5

Trying to be creative, but unfortunately for White it doesn't work. Black can take this rook under the right circumstances.

His only chance was 17.dxe5 ♗xe5 18.♖f3 ♗g6 19.♘d4, although Black still has a very good position after 19...♗e4.

17...♗g6 18.♕d3 ♕e7

Now everything collapses, and all tactics favour Black.

Tarvisio 2017

1	Aryan Tari	IGM NOR	2581	8½
2	Manuel Petrosyan	IGM ARM	2554	8½
3	Ar.Chithambaram Vr.	IGM IND	2572	8½
4	Ra. Praggnanandhaa	IM IND	2509	8
5	Jorden van Foreest	IGM NED	2616	8
6	Alexey Sorokin	FM RUS	2483	8
7	Murali Karthikeyan	IGM IND	2578	8
8	Semen Lomasov	IM RUS	2490	7½
9	Kirill Alekseenko	IGM RUS	2563	7½
10	Xu Xiangyu	IM CHN	2543	7½
11	Liu Yan	FM CHN	2422	7½
12	Bai Jinshi	IGM CHN	2553	7½
13	Alexander Triapishko	IM RUS	2508	7½
14	Tran Tuan Minh	IGM VIE	2538	7½
15	Alexey Sarana	IGM RUS	2543	7½
16	Haik M. Martirosyan	IGM ARM	2561	7½
17	Rasmus Svane	IGM GER	2587	7½
18	Ori Kobo	IGM ISR	2460	7
19	Grigoriy Oparin	IGM RUS	2606	7
20	Shardul Gagare	IGM IND	2482	7
21	Awonder Liang	IGM USA	2558	7
22	Evgeny Zanan	IM ISR	2471	7
	148 players, 11 rounds			

19.dxe5 ♘xe5 20.♕e3 White won't survive after 20.♗xe5 ♗xe5 21.♕d2 ♗xf5 22.gxf5 ♖ae8 either.

20...♗xf5 21.gxf5

21...♕xg5!

This is what Oparin had missed when he went for 20.♕e3. It was definitely not his day!

22.♘f4 ♖ae8

Bringing the last piece to the party.

23.♕e2

White has no time for 23.♕xa7 h5! 24.♘e6 ♖xe6 25.fxe6 h4 26.e7 ♖e8, and it's game over.

23...♘g6 24.♘e6

24...♘f4!!

I was extremely happy with this move, because I saw that after 23.♕e2 it would win on the spot. If it wasn't for this move, White would still be able to put up a fight. The king on g1 makes everything work for Black and he gets an endgame with a lot of extra material.

25.♕g4

Because 25.♘xg5 ♘xh3+ (or 25...♘xe2+ 26.♔h1 ♘xg3+ 27.hxg3 ♖e3) 26.♘xh3 ♖xe2 is hopeless for White.

25...♘xh3+ 26.♕xh3 ♕xf5

White resigned. ∎

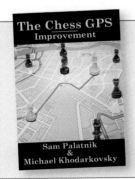

Bill Lombardy at the 1985 OHRA
Tournament in Amsterdam.

In Memoriam, for
Better and for Worse

Bill Lombardy (1937-2017)

Grandmaster William ('Bill') Lombardy passed away in California
on October 13 at the age of 79. Lombardy was the first ever
American to win the Junior World Championship (11-0!) in 1957 and
he was the last survivor of the dominant group of American players
of the 50's and 60's, which included Larry Evans, Robert Byrne,
Samuel Reshevsky, and of course Bobby Fischer. **MARK WIEDER**
remembers an old friend, his triumphs and his tragedy. A complex
personality, increasingly embittered and hard to deal with, but with a

Bill Lombardy was born on December 4, 1937. He grew up in the Bronx, in New York City, and frequented the chess tables in local parks. One of the men there had been clipping chess columns from *The New York Times* and other papers for years and gave young Bill the entire collection. Bill stated that playing over these games opened his mind to the game. The result was the unleashing of a great natural talent.

In his mid-teens, Bill found his way to the Brooklyn home of John ('Jack') Collins, a fairly strong player confined all his life to a wheelchair. Along with Jack's sister Ethel, a nurse and also Jack's caretaker, their home was an open house to up-and-coming young players for decades. Beside Lombardy, the regulars of that era included Robert

Junior World Champion Bill Lombardy, the first American to win that title.

and Donald Byrne, Raymond Weinstein and one Robert James Fischer. Most if not all of these players were much stronger than Jack by the time they began frequenting the Collins home, but they found support in the form of the personal warmth of Ethel and Jack, good food, a great chess library, and each other. The World Chess Hall of Fame in St. Louis has exhibited the chess table and the furniture from this home where Lombardy and Fischer spent many hours analysing with Collins.

Crushing win

Although six years older than Fischer, Bill soon found himself moving from the shadow of the older Reshevsky

to that of his brilliant young friend. While Fischer never chose to play in the World Junior Championship, Bill was the US representative in 1957, scoring a perfect and never-duplicated 11-0 result. It was also the first official world chess title of any kind by an American. Bill's crushing win, with Black, over the event's runner-up, is a nice little gem, highlighted by the quiet 15...a6 backing up the queen sacrifice by depriving White's queen of the b5-square.

Mathias Gerusel
William Lombardy
Toronto 1957
Nimzo-Indian Defence,
Classical Variation

1.d4 ♘f6 2.c4 e6 3.♘c3 ♗b4 4.♕c2 ♘c6 5.♘f3 d5 6.a3 ♗xc3+ 7.♕xc3 ♘e4 8.♕c2 e5!
In his book *Understanding Chess*, Lombardy wrote: 'In my preparations I had the feeling that Gerusel would wander into this gambit. I was committed to proceed as planned. Anything else certainly leads to White's superiority.'
9.dxe5 ♗f5 10.♕a4 0-0 11.♗e3 d4 12.♖d1?

He should have moved the bishop or castled queenside. This allows a devastating queen sacrifice.
12...dxe3! 13.♖xd8 exf2+ 14.♔d1 ♖fxd8+ 15.♔c1 a6! Threatening to win the queen with 16...♘c5.
16.♕b3 ♘c5 17.♕c3 ♘a5! 18.e4 ♘ab3+ 0-1.

In 1960 there was another memorable highlight in his career. In Leningrad,

Bill played second board for the victorious US Student team, winning a gold medal and also his individual game (again with Black) against Boris Spassky, who would become World Champion nine years later. These tournaments were a big deal in their time.

Boris Spassky
William Lombardy
Leningrad 1960
Sicilian Defence, Najdorf Variation

1.e4 c5 2.♘f3 d6 3.d4 cxd4 4.♘xd4 ♘f6 5.♘c3 a6 6.♗g5 ♘bd7 7.♗c4 ♕a5 8.♕d2 e6 9.0-0 ♗e7 10.a3 h6 11.♗e3 ♘e5 12.♗a2 ♕c7 13.♕e2 b5 14.f4?! ♘eg4! 15.h3?
Better was 15.♔h1, removing the king from the g1-a7 diagonal.
15...♘xe3 16.♕xe3 0-0 17.♖ae1 e5!

As Lombardy explained: Black has the bishop pair and a safer king, and now he starts to seize control of the dark squares.
18.♘f5 ♗xf5 19.exf5 d5! 20.♕xe5 ♗d6 21.♕e2 ♗xa3!

22.♘d1? This loses a piece 'to a well-concealed trap'.

White is lost after 22.bxa3 ♕xc3 23.♖f3 ♕b2 24.♗b1 ♖fe8. Lombardy believed that going for an opposite-coloured bishops ending was White's best chance: 22.♘xd5 ♕c5+ 23.♔f2 ♕xf2+ 24.♔xf2 ♗xb2 25.♖d1 ♘xd5 26.♗xd5 ♖ac8 27.♖d2 ♗c3 28.♖d3 ♗f6 29.♖d2 a5, although he thought this should be lost as well.

22...♖ae8 23.♕f3 ♗c5+ 24.♔h1 ♖xe1 25.♖xe1 ♕a5! 'This double attack ends the resistance.'

26.♘c3 ♗b4 27.♘xd5 ♕xa2 28.♘xf6+ He should have tried 28.♘xb4 ♕xb2 29.♘xa6.

28...gxf6 29.♕c6 ♕c4 0-1.

Fischer-Spassky

Bill's decision in the early 60's to enter the seminary and become a Roman Catholic priest certainly impacted his chess career. No one can expect to devote that kind of time in their twenties to another profession without an impact on their chess. He still found time to play from time to time, winning or tying for first in three US Opens from 1963 to 1975.

And so it was that in 1972, when Fischer played Spassky for the World Championship in Reykjavik, Fischer chose Lombardy as his 'second'.

The job of a second includes dealing with the press, the organizers, the federation and arbiters, analysing adjourned positions (a bygone art), reacting to opening surprises, and above all providing psychological support and friendship to the player. This latter task, in the case of Fischer, was the equivalent of living in a minefield, trying to keep the volatile challenger from blowing up the match at every turn.

It was in this role that Lombardy became known to the public outside chess, up to being played by actor Peter Sarsgaard in the 2015 movie *Pawn Sacrifice*.

There are many versions of Lombardy's actual role during this tumultuous match. We do know that after losing the first game and forfeiting the second, Fischer was somehow convinced to continue playing, to the amazement of pretty much everyone in the world. And for sure, the whole world was watching, whether they knew a pawn from a rook or not.

From getting Fischer to board the plane to Iceland to start the match, to get him to continue the match after the forfeit and play to the end, and to play incredibly well in adjourned positions, Lombardy must receive considerable credit as a stabilizing force. Bill told me that in the car after Fischer's first-round loss, Bill pointed out a saving line in the ending that Bobby had overlooked. 'Oh my God, I'm a fish!' was Fischer's reply upon visualizing the position. It turned out the idea did not actually work, but it is stunning to think Fischer could lose his self-confidence even momentarily given his dominance over his peers at the time.

(Editorial note: What exactly Lombardy's role was in Reykjavik we will never know for sure. In *Understanding Chess*, Lombardy himself

> 'The actress came out to say hello, clearly surprised that her character corresponded to a real life person, not to mention a rather stout former priest.'

writes: 'Suffice to say, I was the only person on the intimate inside during that Match of the Century. I chose to say very little because I do not delight in satisfying idle curiosity! As for my "uselessness" on the technical side of chess at Reykjavik, let me point out

Bill Lombardy as seen by Rupert van der Linden in 1982.

that there were 14 adjourned games. Bobby and I worked together on those adjourned positions without making a single error!' This claim seems to be in contrast with, for instance, what American star photographer Harry Benson – who had gained Fischer's trust and spent many hours with him in Iceland – told us in an interview (see New In Chess 2011/4): 'He hated Lombardy. (...) He said: "Lombardy depresses me." Lombardy was going for a walk and asked him to come along for a walk. "OK", Bobby said, "We're leaving at one o'clock." And Bobby would leave at 12.')

Losing his religion

I first met Lombardy at the Bar Point, a bygone New York City games club, in the late 70's. We played two casual games. In the first I thought I was winning with a double attack when a surprising defensive resource destroyed my position. In the second game, my Exchange Variation Lopez was crushed. 'This isn't really your thing,' said my opponent about my handling of the white pieces. Sure enough, I was experimenting in that game. I only then recognized who I'd been playing. Bill had already left the priesthood, having become disillusioned with the Church's bureau-cracy. Soon thereafter he met Louise van Valen, his future wife, while providing commentary as Guest Grandmaster at the 1982 Interpolis tournament in her home town of Tilburg in the Netherlands.

We became close enough friends that when Bill and Louise's son Raymond was born, I was in the bedroom for the birth with Bill, Louise, and their midwife. A few months later when Bill and Louise needed to attend to Bill's dying father in the Bronx, I was called upon to babysit Raymond. The apartment from which Bill was famously evicted last year was in fact the apartment I grew up in; when my parents moved out in the 80's, we made arrange-ments with the landlord for Bill to take over their two bedroom space in the same complex.

When the musical *Chess* was playing on Broadway in New York in the mid-80's, I attended with Bill. The show is (very) loosely based on the Fischer-Spassky match. The American player is abrasive and self-centred, the Russian polite and sympathetic. The American's second is also his girlfriend, who in the course of the play falls in love with the Russian (I did say *very* loosely). When the show ended, a man sitting right in front of us turned to us and asked, 'Who was Fischer's second in Iceland?', to which Lombardy answered, 'I was.' Think of the odds of this happening. The man asking, who was obviously somewhat chess aware, then recognized Lombardy from magazine photos and was liter-ally jumping up and down. Bill and I then went to the stage door and sent word to the actress who played the second, asking if she'd like to come out and meet the person she portrays. She came out to say hello, clearly surprised that the play was in any way based on real events or that her character corresponded to a real life person, not to mention a rather stout former priest.

Ted Field

Bill was always especially kind to lower rated players, answering their questions and offering support. And so when in the late 1980's the famous writer Jerzy Kosinski was looking for a chess coach for his wealthy friend Ted Field, an elderly woman at the Manhattan Chess Club who Bill had treated well directed Kosinski to Bill. Field was a billionaire and an heir to the Marshall Field department store fortune. Field's family fortune dates back to the 1860's, and among the elder Field's 'inventions' were the idea of letting customers return merchandise without question, and to create a luxurious and beautiful space where the customers would be willing to pay premium prices, just to enjoy the experience. For Lombardy, it was a rare case of a good deed going unpunished.

Bill began working with Field during one of the latter's visits to New York at the Waldorf Astoria. They weren't lessons so much as playing sessions, since Field was not terribly receptive to coaching and hoped to eventually win a game against Bill (he never did). Ted asked what Bill's rate was after the first session of about four hours. I think Bill asked for $125 an hour. Ted wrote a check for $25,000 and told Bill to take this on account for future sessions, and that he wanted Bill to be available and not have to worry about money.

Bill introduced me to Ted, and I was lucky enough to be invited many times to Field's spectacular residences in Aspen, Beverly Hills, and Malibu. Bill also got to visit Field's ranch in Santa Barbara and travelled Europe for a time with Field and his entou-rage. Together we hobnobbed with the elite of Hollywood and politics, an exciting time neither Bill nor I could have ever foreseen being part of our lives. We were very well-treated by these luminaries since we had already passed muster with one of their own, who behind the scenes was a great power in the film and music indus-

Bill Lombardy

A short timeline

Born: December 4, 1937, in New York
1954:   Wins New York State Champi-onship.
1957:   World Junior Champion with perfect 11/11 score.
1960:   First board US team that wins World Student Team Champi-onship in Leningrad. Defeats Spassky.
1960:   International Grandmaster.
1960/61: Second behind Fischer in US Championship.
1961:   Retires from tournament chess and enters Roman Catholic seminary.
1963:   Shared first in US Open.
1967:   Ordained as Roman Catholic priest.
1969:   Ties for 2nd with Hort in Monte Carlo.
1972:   Second of Fischer in Match of the Century.
1976:   Member of US team that wins Haifa Olympiad.
Early 1980s: Renounces his priesthood, marries and has a son.
1982:   Shared first in Caracas.
2011:   Publishes autobiographical games collection *Understanding Chess*.
2016:   Evicted from his New York apartment, homeless.
2017, October 13: Dies in California

tries. Among those we socialized with were actors Michael Douglas, Don Johnson and Melanie Griffith, and musicians Paul Simon, John Denver, Sting, Bonnie Raitt, and Don Henley. There was one visitor who insisted on bringing his own security into Field's residences, despite Field's extensive personal cadre of 20-25 bodyguards. This visitor explained that his guards were to protect himself and his family from his own brother, a very dangerous man named... Osama bin Laden.

Spassky and Fischer again

During a Christmas and New Year's period in Aspen, Bill was shocked to find in attendance additional chess stars who had been invited by Ted Field: Boris Spassky, Lev Alburt, and Larry Kaufman. Bill felt understandably put upon that suddenly all these other masters were rivalling him for the attentions of his great padrone. Although Spassky has recently said some unkind things about Lombardy in connection with the Fischer match, the two were very friendly during this stretch, and I felt privileged to get to know Spassky – I even took him skiing. Spassky commented at the time about Bill's chess: 'Oh, he can bite anybody! His only flaw is that he sometimes underestimates the value of the initiative.'

Field wanted to meet Fischer, then living in Pasadena, California. Fischer would not speak to Lombardy, unhappy that Bill had 'enriched' himself by writing a glowing article about Bobby after the match for *Sports Illustrated*. But Spassky was able to approach Bobby, who wanted $10,000 to visit Field. Spassky had a good feel for negotiating with Bobby and after 'reluctantly' agreeing to terms like prepayment and a limousine, Bobby was driven to Field's estate in Beverly Hills. Bobby was very excited at the time about his invention of the time-add (or time delay) chess clock and talked about it to Field. But Bobby soon diverged into an anti-Semitic rant, which Field, although not Jewish, would have no part of, and Fischer was sent on his way much earlier than the agreed upon endpoint of the session.

Field sponsored the New York half of the 1990 World Championship match between Karpov and Kasparov and promised Lombardy an important, although unspecified, role in the proceedings. At the end of the twelve New York games, Bill went over the games with Kasparov (while Ted Field watched) and commented later as to Garry's incredible objectivity in assessing the positions. But Bill felt that Field had reneged on his promise of a role in the match, and became disillusioned with the relationship. The two severed their ties shortly thereafter and Field's interest in chess eventually went completely by the wayside.

During these New York games, the great Miguel Najdorf visited the match and accompanied Bill and me to dinner one night at the recently closed Carnegie Deli in New York. We went back to Bill's apartment and Bill and I took turns playing blitz against Najdorf. During one of the games, Najdorf played a move against me and hit the clock. A few moments later he undid the move and played a different move. 'Don Miguel?' I asked quizzically. I found an index finger sharply pointed at me as the voice boomed: 'When you are 80 years old and Grandmaster, you can also take back move against patzer. Najdorf plays for beauty!' I sheepishly continued my path to oblivion, destroyed as expected on the Black side of… a Najdorf Sicilian.

During the evening Najdorf won one game against Bill and screamed 'Haha, BILLY!!' He was so proud to take the measure of Lombardy at the age of 80.

Frequent diatribes

Bill thought he had found an annuity in Field and that he would never have to worry about money again. Outside of some funds generated by sporadic lessons, lectures, and writing, Bill lived out his life over the next 25+ years by gradually exhausting the savings accumulated from the billionaire's largesse, and by late 2016 he was, tragically, homeless on the streets of New York.

I found it difficult to maintain my close relationship with Bill beginning in the mid-90's. His marriage ended around 1992 and Louise and their son moved to Holland. It seemed that Bill became more and more like Bobby Fischer as he got older. He was terribly embittered, increasingly hard to deal with, and almost impossible to extract oneself from once he got into one of his frequent diatribes about the injustices of the chess world, and the world at large. He resented that so many players with much less talent made a good living teaching and writing about chess, overlooking that these same people also promoted themselves with hard work and good public relations. By comparison, I learned of a time when a strong young student was brought to Bill's apartment for a lesson late on an afternoon, only to be greeted by Bill in a bathrobe. Anyone familiar with his Bohemian lifestyle would recognize that Bill had certainly still been asleep from the night before when awakened by the arrival of the student. But to the mother of the student, the inappropriate attire mandated the end of the sessions.

I saw Bill at a fund raiser in New York in 2010 in support of the Karpov candidacy for FIDE President, an event attended and supported by Garry Kasparov(!) and Magnus Carlsen. Bill was anxious to speak with Karpov, whom he held in great personal regard. But he would also say that having seen Fischer, it was hard to be impressed by anyone else. A year later I attended the wake for Jack Collins, but their relationship hadn't survived and Bill did not show up.

Bill was not an easy person to help, as many people have noted. He used to go to a dentist, a long-time friend of mine. Bill needed an enormous amount of expensive dental work, far beyond his financial means. The dentist told Bill that an oral surgeon he knew would do all the work for free in consideration of Bill's financial limitations and his great chess talent. (In fact, I had made an arrangement with the surgeon that I would pay the bills in secret.) But Bill never called the surgeon.

Playing like a house

The last time I saw and spoke to Bill was in the chess area of Washington Square Park a couple of months before his death. We spoke a little along with some of the park players. Bill's eyesight had deteriorated and I wasn't sure if he recognized me. He had a shopping cart of belongings, as is common among the homeless in New York.

Here is perhaps Lombardy's greatest game, another win with Black against a great player. In the middle of this game, Fischer looked at the board and commented to another player, 'Lombardy is playing like a house!'

Samuel Reshevsky
William Lombardy
New York 1957
King's Indian Defence

1.d4 ♘f6 2.c4 g6 3.♘c3 ♗g7 4.e4 d6 5.♗e2 0-0 6.♘f3 e5 7.0-0 ♘c6 8.d5 ♘e7 9.♘e1 ♘d7 10.♘d3 f5 11.f3 f4 12.♗d2 g5 13.♖c1 ♘g6 14.♘b5 a6 15.♘a3 ♘f6 16.c5 g4 17.cxd6 cxd6 18.♘c4 g3 19.h3 ♗xh3!

Bill Lombardy on June 5 of this year at Cardinal Cooke Rehab Hospital in New York, where he spent a few weeks after being assaulted while living on the street.

Lombardy: 'This may have come as a shock to Sammy, who had announced to the players in the outer room of the Manhattan Chess Club that he 'was killing' me!'

20.gxh3 ♕d7 21.♘f2 gxf2+ 22.♔h2 ♕e7! 23.♖xf2 ♘h5 24.♗b4 ♖ad8 25.♕d3 ♘h4 26.♖g1 ♘g3 27.♗f1 ♖f6 28.♖c2 ♖g6 29.♗e1 ♗h6! Preventing the capture on g3, as the bishop would come to f4.

30.♘b6 ♔h8 31.♗g2 ♖dg8 32.♖c8 ♗f8!

Lombardy: 'Naturally Black retains his rook for the attack. The battle will be decided on the g-file. Verdun is surrounded! In chess the superior force prevails!'

33.♖c2 ♕g7

Lombardy: 'Tripling heavy pieces on the file prepares for the slaughter. I believe Sammy might well have resigned here, were his rival one of the world class candidates. But Sammy was obliged to continue, since he retained hopes of catching Bobby for the title.'

34.♘a8 ♕h6 35.♗f1 ♘xf1+ 36.♖xf1 ♕g7 37.♕e2 ♖g2+ 38.♕xg2 ♘xg2 39.♖g1 ♘xe1 40.♖xg7 ♗xg7 0-1.

I'll always remember and miss the good years being friends with Bill, watching him clarify complex chess positions with astonishing ease, hearing his stories about the greats of the game, especially Fischer, whom he regarded only with affection and positive memories. ∎

Mark A Wieder, is an American chess player and chess lover from the New York City area and member of the Marshall Chess Club. He is the owner and founder of a computer software development company.

A Refined Owen's Defence

Jeroen Bosch

1...b6!?

'**Strong grandmasters avoid playing 1...b6 against 1.e4 and 1.d4.**'

After a disappointing exit in the third round of the Tbilisi World Cup, Magnus Carlsen won the Isle of Man open tournament. Unshared first with 7½ out of 9 and a 2900 performance speak for themselves. The great thing about the Norwegian's opening strategy was that he always kept his opponents guessing. Thus his choice ranged from absolute mainstream lines (Granda, Caruana and Nakamura) to Tiger's Modern (Perelshteyn), 1.♘f3 c5 2.c3!? (Xiong), the SOS Pirc-Nimzowitsch hybrid from New In Chess 2017/6 (Kasimdzhanov), to a clever move order to reach Owen's Defence in the present game.

Pavel Eljanov
Magnus Carlsen
Douglas 2017

1.♘f3 b6!? As Carlsen explained after the game, he had prepared mainly for 1.d4 and 1.e4, so that 1.♘f3 came as a bit of a surprise. He pointed out that if you want to go for Owen's Defence, this may well be Black's best move order option. It is, in fact, a move order that had already been used by the likes of Smyslov, Larsen and Ivanchuk.
Owen's Defence proper arises after 1.e4 b6 2.d4 ♗b7. The Reverend John Owen played this in the 19th century, and 1...b6 deservedly bears his name. The Reverend's main claim to fame is probably his win over Paul Morphy in a casual game in London 1858. Tony

Miles used to play 1...b6, although he mainly favoured this move against the English Opening, which funnily enough becomes the English Defence after 1.c4 b6. In recent years, Eugenio Torre's occasional use of 1...b6 is a thing of note.
On the whole, however, strong grandmasters avoid playing 1...b6 against 1.e4 and 1.d4. There are several reasons for this reluctance: 1.e4 b6 2.d4 ♗b7 3.♗d3 (another decent line is 3.♘c3 e6 4.a3) 3...♘f6

4.♘c3 (here 4.♕e2 is flexible, since it avoids the pinning of the knight with a later ...♗b4 after 4...e6 5.♘f3 c5 6.c3! – instead, 4...♘c6!? 5.c3 e5 is a favourite line of GM Pavel Blatny's – and Torre plays it, too – a line for the true believers) 4...e6 5.♘f3 (good alternatives are 5.a3 and 5.♘ge2!?) 5...♗b4, and we have reached the game position, but as we have seen, White has some nasty alternatives in the regular move order. **2.e4 ♗b7 3.♘c3 e6**

4.d4 ♗b4 Developing bishops before knights is Black's best bet here, exerting pressure on White's pawn centre. This could be considered the main line of Owen's Defence, since White develops normally (knights to their natural squares, bishop to d3 and castling kingside), but as I have pointed out, there are 'nastier' alternatives along the way. In fact, I believe that reaching this position as Black should be considered a success when you start out with 1...b6.

5.♗d3 ♘f6 Via exactly the same move order as Eljanov-Carlsen, the game Garcia Gonzales-Larsen (Orense 1975) also reached this position, after which the great Dane went his own way with 5...♗xc3+ 6.bxc3 ♘e7 7.0-0 d6 8.♖e1 ♘d7 9.e5! dxe5 10.♘xe5 ♘xe5 11.♖xe5 ♘g6 12.♖h5. White is better at this stage, but Larsen won.

6.♕e2 White has several alternatives, but none of them are stronger than Eljanov's queen move.
■ Sharp play arises after the pawn sacrifice 6.e5 ♘e4 7.0-0!?.
Having said A, White must go through with B (the pawn sac). No good is 7.♗xe4 ♗xe4 8.0-0 ♗xc3!

9.bxc3 0-0 10.♕e2 ♗b7 11.♗a3 d6 12.♕e3 ♕d7 (12...♖e8) 13.♖fe1, Pogonina-Ding Liren, St. Petersburg 2012, and now, besides the game continuation 13...♘c6, also good is 13...♕a4 14.c4 ♗xf3 15.♕xf3 ♘c6.

If you want to take up this line as Black, you are well-advised to study this particular line, in which concrete variations are essential.
7...♘xc3 8.bxc3 ♗xc3 (not 8...♗e7, as 9.♘d2 planning ♕g4 looks better for White) 9.♖b1 ♘c6 (this seems to lead to forced draw – Bauer gives 9...♗d5!? as an attempt to avoid the draw and play for more: 10.♗g5 ♕c8 11.♗d2 ♗xd2 12.♘xd2 ♗xa2 13.♖a1 ♗d5 14.c4, Akhayan-Tew, Kallithea 2008 – in my opinion, White has scary compensation) 10.♖b3 ♗xd4 (10...♗b4!?) 11.♘xd4 ♘xd4 12.♕g4

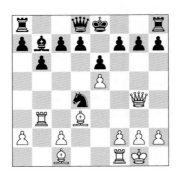

and now there is no longer any choice:
12...♘xb3 13.♕xg7 ♘xc1 (13...♖f8? 14.♗g5, winning) 14.♕xh8+ ♔e7 15.♕f6+ ♔e8 16.♕h8+ ♔e7 ½-½, Joecks-Weyrich, Germany 1994.
■ Black should be fine after 6.♗g5 h6 7.♗xf6 ♗xc3+ (7...♕xf6 8.♕d2). Note how often Black should voluntarily take on c3 to inflict damage on

White's pawn structure. 8.bxc3 ♕xf6 9.0-0 d6 10.♘d2 (10.♗b5+ ♘d7 11.♕d3 ♘e7 12.♗a6 ♗xa6 13.♕xa6 0-0 14.♖fe1 c5 was slightly better for Black in Larsen-Timman, Tilburg 1980) 10...e5 (a fairly common position that seems healthy enough for Black) 11.f4

And now:
– 11...exd4?! 12.e5 dxe5 13.♕h5 g6 14.♕e2 ♘c6 15.fxe5 ♕e7 16.e6 f5 17.♘b3 0-0-0 favoured Black in Ionescu-Smyslov, Sochi 1986 (but White won!). However, instead of 13.♕h5 White should just continue 13.fxe5!, which has scored tremendously in practice.
– 11...♕e7 12.♕g4! 0-0 13.♘c4 ♘d7 (13...f5 14.exf5 e4 15.♗e2 ♘d7 16.♘e3±) 14.♘e3 with a dangerous initiative was David-Bauer, Port Barcares 2005.
– Probably best is 11...exf4 12.g3 g5, as first played in Spassky-Miles, Niksic 1983.
■ 6.♘d2 looks a little odd, but Kramnik has played it in a blitz game, so it's worth checking out!

– Here 6...c5!? 7.dxc5 ♘c6!? 8.cxb6 ♗xc3 9.bxc3 axb6 is suggested by

Lakdawala as a Houdini approach in his book on 1...b6 (*1...b6: Move by Move*, Everyman 2014). Black, with his better structure, has (some) compensation for the pawn.

– 6...d5 7.e5 ♘e4! (7...♘fd7?! 8.0-0 c5 9.♕g4! g6 10.♘b5 cxd4 11.♘f3 ♘c6 was Kramnik-Andreikin, Moscow blitz 2013 – both 12.♗g5 and 12.♗h6 are strong now) 8.♕g4 ♔f8! 9.♗xe4 (similarly, 9.♘cxe4 dxe4 10.♗c4 h5 also gives counterplay) 9...dxe4 10.♘cxe4 h5 (the alternative is 10...♕d5!? 11.0-0 h5)

11.♕f4! (11.♕e2?! ♗xd2+ 12.♗xd2 ♕xd4; 11.♕f3? ♗xd2+!; 11.♕g5? ♘c6! 12.♕xd8+ ♖xd8 13.c3 ♘xd4!) 11...♗xd2+ 12.♘xd2! ♘c6 (worse is 12...♕xg2?! 13.♖g1 ♗b7 14.c3 ♘c6 15.b3 ♘e7 16.♗a3±, Saint Amour-Garibaldi, email 2002) 13.c3 ♘e7 14.♘f3 ♗g6 15.♕e3 h4, and due to the powerful bishop on the long diagonal Black had some compensation for the pawn in Buss-Filipovic, Switzerland 2004.

– I think that Black should consider 6...d6!?, intending something like 7.0-0 (7.♘cb1!? d5!) 7...0-0 8.a3 ♗xc3 9.bxc3 ♘bd7.

6...d5!

7.exd5 In a way, this is a concession (giving up your pawn centre), but it is nevertheless best at this stage.

Here 7.♗g5?! is no good in view of 7...dxe4 8.♗xe4 ♗xe4 9.♗xf6, and now 9...♕d5!.

Please note that 7.♘d2?! is no good either, since Black has 7...♘c6! 8.exd5 (8.e5? ♘xd4) 8...♘xd5 9.♘xd5 ♘xd4.

Black meets 7.e5 with 7...♘e4, after which it is White who has to pay attention. Best now is 8.0-0! ♘xc3 9.bxc3 ♗xc3 10.♖b1 ♘c6!

White's main argument for having sacrificed a pawn is his lead in development, so the text is correct: developing and attacking d4. Three examples:

– 11.♗e3 ♘b4 12.♗b5+ c6 13.a3 cxb5 14.axb4 ♕d7 15.♖b3 ♖c8 16.♗d2 ♗xd2 17.♕xd2 ♖c4 18.♖a1 a6∓, Radjabov-Ivanchuk, Eilat 2012.

– 11.♖d1 ♕d7 12.a3 ♘xd4 13.♘xd4 ♗xd4 14.c3 ♗xc3 15.♖bc1 ♗a5 16.♖xc7 was imaginative, but Black was still better after 16...♕xc7 17.♖c1 ♕xc1+ 18.♗xc1 0-0-0!, Pavlovic-Minasian, Moscow 2008.

– 11.♕e3 ♗b4 12.♕f4 h6 13.♗b5 ♗e7 14.♕g4 g6 15.c3 ♕d7 16.♘e1 a6 17.♗a4 b5, and White had insufficient compensation for the pawn in Nakamura-Gareev, St. Louis 2015.

7...♕xd5!?

Even in an obscure opening, Carlsen does not play the most obvious move! In Thomas Kapitaniak's old book *b6!* (The Chess Player, 1982) 7...♘xd5 is given as the main line and 7...♕xd5 as a small note. In the past couple of decades, taking with the queen has become more customary, though. It's a matter of taste mainly.

So, also playable is 7...♘xd5!? 8.♗d2 (8.0-0!?) 8...♘xc3 (very safe is the boring 8...♘d7 9.♘xd5 ♗xd2+ 10.♘xd2 ♕xd5 11.0-0 0-0 12.c4 ♗b7, and White has basically nothing in this French Rubinstein-like position, Rogers-Miles, Auckland 1992) 9.bxc3 ♗e7

10.0-0 (one reason why Carlsen may have preferred playing 7...♕xd5 might be that White can force a draw with 10.♘e5 0-0 – not 10...♘d7? 11.♗b5± – 11.♕h5 g6 – 11...f5 12.0-0± – 12.♘xg6 fxg6 13.♗xg6 hxg6 14.♕xg6+) 10...0-0 11.♘e5 ♘d7 12.f4 c5, and here Black is at least even.

8.0-0

White can keep his structure intact with 8.♗d2 ♗xc3 9.♗xc3, but cannot get an advantage in this way. Black has very nice control of the central light squares. 9...♘bd7 10.♗b4 (Black is very comfortable after 10.0-0 ♘e4! 11.♗xe4 ♕xe4 12.♕xe4 ♗xe4 13.♘e1 ♘f6 14.f3 ♗g6, Mikhalchishin-Gurgenidze, Volgodonsk 1981) 10...♕h5! 11.0-0-0 0-0-0 12.♗e7 ♖de8 13.♗xf6 ♘xf6 14.♗a6 was equal in Moreno Perales-Burmakin, Balaguer 2006.

8...♗xc3 9.bxc3 ♘bd7

Alternatively, Black can castle first. After 9...0-0 10.♗f4 it makes sense to study a game by the author of *Play 1... b6* (Everyman, 2005): 10...♖c8 11.♖fe1 c5 12.dxc5 ♕xc5 13.c4 ♘bd7 14.a4 ♖e8 (14...a5 is recommended by Lakdawala, and this is in style with how Carlsen plays in the main game. It fixes pawn a4 as a weakness) 15.a5 e5 16.♗e3 ♕c7 17.♗f5?! bxa5! 18.♗d2, Bareev-Bauer, Enghien-les-Bains 2001, and now 18... a4! 19.♖xa4 ♘b6 20.♖b4 g6 21.♗h3 ♗a6 is much better for Black.

10.c4 Here 10.♖e1 ♕h5 11.a4 ♗xf3!? 12.gxf3 0-0 13.♔h1 ♖fe8 is pretty unclear, Sherzer-Oliveira, Philadelphia 1993.

10...♕h5

We have already seen that the queen is well-placed on this square. Black's general plan is pretty simple, too. He wants to castle and place his rooks on the c- and d-files, when in combination with ...c7-c5 he will put pressure on White's centre.

11.♗f4 ♖c8 Here the earlier Vukovic-Velimirovic, Niksic 1994, was agreed drawn after 11...c5.

11...♗xf3 12.gxf3 ♖c8 is met by 13.♔h1, and the bishops and the open g-file may work in White's favour.

12.a4 a5

Carlsen called this very ambitious. He wants to fix the a-pawn as a weakness. It works like a dream in the game. A plausible continuation after 12...0-0 13.a5 would be 13...c5 14.axb6 axb6 15.c3, when Black does best to thwart White's initiative with 15...♗xf3! 16.♕xf3 ♕xf3 17.gxf3 e5!, when 18.♗xe5 ♘xe5 19.dxe5 ♘h5 leads to a kind of fortress.

13.♖ab1 13.♘d2 ♕xe2 14.♗xe2 is

the type of thing that White can do, according to Carlsen, who felt that White would be a tad better but no more. **13...0-0 14.♖b5 c5**

15.dxc5

Critical, according to Carlsen, was 15.♗d6 ♗c6, when after 16.♗xf8 he hesitated between the exchange sacrifice 16...♔xf8, which provides sufficient compensation after 17.♖bb1 ♗xf3 18.♕xf3 ♕xf3 19.gxf3 cxd4, and 16...♗xb5, which is also balanced after 17.♗xc5 (17.♗xg7 ♔xg7 18.cxb5 cxd4) 17...♖xc4! 18.♗xc4 bxc5 19.♗a6.

If White plays the strengthening 15.c3, Black just continues 15...♗c6, when pawn a4 drops unless White decides to sac the exchange with 16.♖fb1 ♗xb5 17.♖xb5, when the bishop pair is ample compensation for an unclear or equal game.

15...♖xc5 16.♗d6 ♖xb5 17.cxb5?! Correct was 17.axb5, which is perhaps surprising. The thing is that pawn a4 is just a weakness.

17...♖c8 Now Black is better. Carlsen pointed out that the bishop pair is of no value here, because White's light-squared bishop is so bad.

18.c4 ♘c5

19.♗c2 The bishop is no longer an attacking piece but a passive defender of a weak pawn. Black's pieces, on the other hand, are all very active.

19...♘ce4 20.♗f4?! This makes matters worse, but the c-pawn drops after 20.♗e5 ♘g5 21.♘d4 ♕xe2 22.♘xe2 ♖xc4.

20...♘c3!∓ 21.♕d3 White loses the endgame arising after 21.♕e5 ♗xf3! 22.♕xc3 ♘d5! 23.♕xf3 ♕xf3 24.gxf3 ♘xf4.

21...♗g4 Also winning is 21...♗xf3 22.gxf3 (22.♕xc3 ♘d5 transposes to the previous note) 22...♕g6+.

22.♗e5 In case of 22.♕xc3 Black has an attractive choice between the prosaic 22...♕xf4 23.♘e5 (23.♘d2) 23...♗g4 24.♘xg4 ♕xg4 25.f3 ♕xc4 and the combinatory 22...♘d5 23.♘e5 ♕xg2+ (23...♗xf4 24.♘xg4 ♘e2+ 25.♔h1 ♘xc3) 24.♔xg2 ♘xf4+ 25.♔g3 ♘e2+ 26.♔h3 ♘xc3.

22...♕xc4 23.♕xc4 ♖xc4

Black has already won a pawn, while a4 remains a weakness. Just as importantly, Black retains the more active pieces, which guarantees an easy win.

24.♗d3 ♖c8 25.♖a1 ♘fd5 26.♘d2 f6 27.♗d6?! ♘b4! 28.♗c4 After 28.♗xb4 axb4 29.♘c4 the passed b-pawn and the extra pawn decide after 29...b3! 30.♘b2 (30.f3 ♖xc4!) 30...♗e4 31.♗xe4 ♖xe4. **28...♘d5 29.♗f1 ♘ba2** Now the a-pawn drops off as well, which is why Eljanov resigned.

We have seen that one of the main lines in Owen's Defence is highly playable for Black, and best reached via an alternative move order. So don't play 1.e4 b6?!, but 1.♘f3 b6!. ∎

For fun & for blood

Magnus Carlsen in a different league in Champions Showdown

The Champions Showdown has rapidly become a popular autumn fixture at the always buzzing Saint Louis Chess Club. Entertainment and experiment are the key words as top stars engage in unusual competitions, this time a mix of time-controls – in four attractive matchups – that had one thing in common: no 'increments' or 'delays'! **ALEJANDRO RAMIREZ** reports from the US Capital of Chess.

The Champions' Showdown has become a staple in the already hectic schedule of the Chess Club and Scholastic Center of Saint Louis. Every November, the club organizes a spectacle that involves the top American players and some world-class guests, and adds a certain twist or unusual element to play.

The Showdown is fully intended to be an experimental tournament that is more for fun than for anything else, except that it has gigantic prize funds.

Last year's experiment introduced a significant portion of the audience to 'delay', a time-control that was new to most Europeans (see New In Chess 2016/8). The eccentricity of delay was successful enough for the organizers of the Grand Chess Tour to incorporate it in their rapid and blitz tournaments without much opposition. Some people fear, or hope, that this year's Showdown might be a premonition of future events. And this year, the experiment was having to

The moment Magnus Carlsen expressed his interest to take part in the Champions Showdown, the St. Louis organizers took action and even allowed him to start two days later than the others. The World Champion didn't disappoint and provided high-level entertainment.

LENNART OOTES

play without increments or delays... Simply a fixed amount of time for the entire game, and if you ran out of time, you simply lost. Just as in the old days.

Incredible prize fund

The experimental nature of the Showdown didn't mean that it was not taken seriously. On the contrary. And for good reasons. Firstly, there was the inclusion of Magnus Carlsen. Everyone knows the difference in attention chess circles give to an event in which the World Champion is playing compared to an event with the rest of the top players (the big exception is if a certain Garry Kasparov is playing, of course). Secondly, there was an incredible prize fund: $400,000 to be divided between eight players for four days of work.

The format of the event was as follows: four individual matches that had nothing to do with each other, played over four days. The first day featured games for which the players got 30 minutes each. In technical terms: G/30. The second day was dedicated to games with 20 minutes' thinking time for each player, in other words G/20. And then there was a G/10 day, and finally a G/5 day. The games were weighted in such

between the Grand Chess Tour, the US Championship and other serious commitments, it is sometimes difficult to fit everything in! The rivals the Americans could pick were already from a relatively small pool, since a

> ## 'Everyone knows the difference in attention chess circles give to an event in which the World Champion is playing.'

a way that every day was worth 24 points, except the first one, which was worth 20. G/30 games were worth 5 points each, G/20 was 4, G/10 3 and G/5 only 2.

The way the players for the four matches were picked was rather unusual. Originally, the tournament was simply going to feature the top Americans, and each one was going to pick one opponent. But the organizers were on a very tight schedule. The Club does its best to juggle all of its high-level tournaments, but

few would decline in order to focus on the Palma de Mallorca Grand Prix as their final shot to qualify to the Candidates', while others had previous commitments.

Finally, the series of matches seemed to be as follows: Hikaru Nakamura chose Veselin Topalov, Fabiano Caruana would face Alexander Grischuk, and Wesley So chose Leinier Dominguez as his opponent. But one way or another, Magnus Carlsen or someone in his team learned of the event, and suddenly

St. Louis 2017 Champions Showdown							
G/5 – 12 rounds – 5 minutes per player for the entire game – 2 points for a win							
1 Hikaru Nakamura	21	1 Fabiano Caruana	17	1 Wesley So	17	1 Magnus Carlsen	17
2 Veselin Topalov	3	2 Alexander Grischuk	7	2 Leinier Dominguez	7	2 Ding Liren	7
G/10 – 8 rounds – 10 minutes per player for the entire game – 3 points for a win							
1 Hikaru Nakamura	12	1 Fabiano Caruana	12	1 Wesley So	15	1 Magnus Carlsen	19½
2 Veselin Topalov	12	2 Alexander Grischuk	12	2 Leinier Dominguez	9	2 Ding Liren	4½
G/20 – 6 rounds – 20 minutes per player for the entire game – 4 points for a win							
1 Hikaru Nakamura	16	1 Alexander Grischuk	14	1 Leinier Dominguez	16	1 Magnus Carlsen	18
2 Veselin Topalov	8	2 Fabiano Caruana	10	2 Wesley So	8	2 Ding Liren	6
G/30 – 4 rounds – 30 minutes per player for the entire game – 5 points for a win							
1 Hikaru Nakamura	12½	1 Fabiano Caruana	10	1 Leinier Dominguez	12½	1 Magnus Carlsen	12½
2 Veselin Topalov	7½	2 Alexander Grischuk	10	2 Wesley So	7½	2 Ding Liren	7½
Total							
1 Hikaru Nakamura	61½	1 Fabiano Caruana	49	1 Wesley So	47½	1 Magnus Carlsen	67
2 Veselin Topalov	30½	2 Alexander Grischuk	43	2 Leinier Dominguez	44½	2 Ding Liren	25

the World Champion was interested in playing! However, the dates didn't quite work, because Carlsen had an exhibition in Hamburg when the event started. Well, no problem: he could start two days late! Now an opponent had to be found. Great credit must be given to Joy Bray and Tony Rich, the people that basically make everything happen at the Club, who managed to find a way to convince China's number one Ding Liren to play in such a way that 24 hours after his last round against Carlsen he would be attending the aforementioned Grand Prix's opening ceremony in Mallorca. One supposes that it helped that he had already qualified for the Candidates' in the recent World Cup in Tbilisi, and no doubt the guaranteed $40,000 if he lost was a good argument to sway him.

The way things were set up made it seem as if the first three matches were a kind of appetizer for the main duel between Ding Liren and Carlsen, but that was never the idea. Indeed, two of the matches were an absolute spectacle, while the remaining two were such bloodbaths that children would be ill-advised to go over the results.

As the commentary trio and the production team were setting up for the live broadcast, many questions were on everyone's minds. What if pieces went flying in serious time-pressure? Would the players actually like this time-control? How many games would be called by an arbiter? Caruana even asked at some point if there would be some kind of gentlemen's agreement on completely drawn positions or whether time would reign supreme. As with all experimental tournaments, things were figured out bit by bit, day by day.

'Broadening my horizons'

It's probably easiest to look at the event as four separate matches, and present them as such.

Nakamura's choice of Topalov was certainly the strangest one of

As Hikaru Nakamura picks up the 'loose' knight on h4, Veselin Topalov can still see the fun of losing a blitz game in which he was a piece up ten moves from the end.

the bunch. Topalov has repeatedly expressed his weakness in faster time-controls, while Nakamura is no longer the teenager that would take joy in flagging everyone on every Internet chess server. His speed is still incredible and his blitz skills are arguably second to only the World Champion's. Naka said during one of his interviews: 'I am trying to experiment a little bit, play a little bit sharper, play things that are a little bit different, and I think that Veselin, from that standpoint, is a very good opponent to play, because he is very sharp tactically and sees many things. I'm trying to broaden my horizons.'

Whatever the reasoning, the match was truly one-sided. The positions on the board gave excellent chances to the former World Champion, but an amazing amount of clear advantages and winning positions either dissipated or turned against him. Despite only being -3 on a traditional scoring system, the -13 of Topalov looked very bad as the time-controls became faster and faster. He truly put up a fight in the G/10, but the G/5 was a massacre. Nakamura clinched

the match after the second game of the fourth day, with the players still having to play 10 more games. If one were to summarize how a great amount of games went, it would be the following snippet:

Hikaru Nakamura
Veselin Topalov
St. Louis 2017 (26)

position after 75...♔g8

After White's capture of the rook Topalov is a piece up. He was low on time, but he actually lost in the play.
76.♘xd7 ♗e5 77.♘xb8 g5 78.hxg5 ♔f7 79.♔f4 ♘d3+ 80.♔e4 ♘e1 81.♘c6 ♘xg2 82.♘e5+ ♔e6 83.♘f3

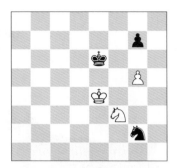

At this point, Topalov reached and grabbed his knight, only to realize that it had no moves. After **83...♘h4 84.♘xh4** Black resigned.

In another game, Topalov gave Nakamura a draw when the American literally had one second left on the clock. Naka proved to be incredibly resourceful and managed to wiggle out of bad positions constantly, like this one:

Veselin Topalov
Hikaru Nakamura
St. Louis 2017 (27)

position after 18...♖xa3

How we got here isn't very important. The fact that White will be an

exchange up is clear, although obviously Black has some initiative on the kingside. These kind of scenarios, with a murky position in which Topalov is clearly winning, always seemed to favour Nakamura.
19.♖xa3 ♘g6 20.g3 f3 21.♗d3 h5 22.♖a8 h4 23.♘b5

The interesting thing about this is that if you put a rook on a8 and a knight on b5, you more or less expect White to play his threat of ♘a7.
23...♔h7
Threateningly, Black intends to advances his pawns...
24.♕c2
But 24.♘a7 simply would have picked up another piece: 24...hxg3 25.hxg3 ♕xd6 26.♖xc8, and Black is very far away from the h3-square. And White can always sacrifice something back on f3.
24...♘h5 25.d7?! ♕xd7 26.♖c1?!
26.♘a7 here or on the previous move was better.
26...hxg3 27.hxg3 ♘gf4
By now Nakamura has managed to muddy the waters a bit.
28.gxf4 ♘xf4 29.♕c7

29...♕e8!
Another expert thing about Nakamura is that once he has equalized, he never looks for a draw, but keeps increasing the complications to find a way to win.
30.♖xc8 ♕h5 31.♖xf8 ♕h3 32.♖h8+ ♔xh8 33.♕c8+ ♔h7 34.♕f5+ ♔h6
In a classical time-control White's move would be obvious. In blitz Topalov breaks.

35.♕xf4+?
After 35.♕e6+ ♘xe6 36.♗f1 ♕h4 37.dxe6 the passed e-pawn and the locked bishop don't allow Black any chances for a real attack.
35...exf4 36.♗f1 ♕h5

Now g3 is inevitable and the dark-squared bishop is a monster.
37.♘d6 g3 38.♘f5+ ♚g5 39.fxg3 fxg3 40.♘xf3+ ♛xf3 41.♗g2 ♗d4+ Black will mate soon, so White resigned.

Caruana upsets blitz specialist

The match between Fabiano Caruana and Alexander Grischuk was far more interesting. The players traded blows constantly: as soon as one scored, the other one retaliated in the next bout. The very first game showcased Grischuk's slow adaptation to the new time-control when he focused on winning the position rather than the clock. Caruana realized what was happening, and stopped looking at the play and just kept moving his king back and forth, even leaving his queen en prise for no reason. His final strange move allowed Grischuk to capture his last piece, a bishop. The magic of modern technology shows that Grischuk's flag fell before he captured the bishop, but the players agreed to a draw anyway.

The arbiters, probably completely unaccustomed to calling things like flags and illegal moves, seemed oblivious to the rules on the first two days. Neither Caruana-Grischuk after this nor Nakamura-Topalov had any big controversies, luckily.

Grischuk was taking the match very seriously, consulting his second, Vladislav Tkachiev, between rounds for improvements. At some point, Caruana decided to experiment with openings, but it didn't always turn out well and sometimes he landed himself in dubious positions:

Alexander Grischuk
Fabiano Caruana
St. Louis 2017 (14)

position after 23.exf5

This is from a G/10 game, with 10 minutes for each player for the complete game. But it doesn't matter how fast the time-control is; this position is terrible for Black. Grischuk continues to play powerful chess, but Caruana is resilient.
23...gxf5 24.♘cb5! ♗xb5 25.cxb5 ♘b4

26.♘xf5! A simple but nice tactic based on the weakness of the rook on d7. **26...♘xb3!** Probably the best move to keep fighting. After 26...exf5 27.♗xc5 there is no hope left for Black. **27.axb3 exf5 28.♗b6 ♖a8**

29.♗xa5?!
29.g4!, opening the diagonal for the bishop on b1, was devastating. Not a natural 'blitz' move, however.
And 29.♛g5 was even stronger.
29...♖xa5 30.♛xb4 ♖a8 31.♛f4 ♖f8 32.♖xd6 ♖xd6 33.♛xd6 ♛xb3

34.♛e6+
These kinds of practical decisions in a blitz or rapid game are very different from classical chess. Grischuk once said that in a blitz game, if you've reached a winning position, it doesn't matter if you win by flagging or playing. Trading queens leads to an endgame Black can probably hold with perfect play, but in practice it is incredibly difficult. Caruana does his best, but eventually falters.
34...♛xe6 35.♖xe6 ♗d4+ 36.♚f1 b6 37.♖d6 ♗c5 38.♖d7 h6 39.♗d3 f4 40.♗h7+ ♚h8 41.♗e4 ♚g8 42.♚e2 ♖f6 43.♗d5+ ♚h8 44.♖d8+ ♖f8 45.♖d7 ♖f6 46.♗c7 ♖d6 47.♗e4

47...♗e3?
The mistake. Now Grischuk advances

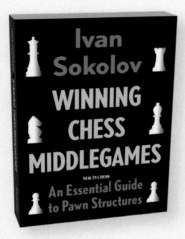
his pawns and, even though he isn't winning by force, without increments it is impossible to hold such a position.

48.g4! ♖d2+ 49.♔e1 ♔g8 50.♖c6 ♖b2 51.♖xh6 ♖xb5 52.h4 ♖b2 53.g5 ♖h2 54.h5 b5 55.♖g6+ ♔f8 56.h6 ♖h5 57.♖f6+ ♔e7 58.h7 ♘d4 59.♖f5 ♖xh7 60.♖xb5 ♖h2 61.♖d5 ♗c3+ 62.♔d1 ♔e6 63.♔c1 ♖g2 64.♖c5 ♗d4 65.♖b5 ♔e7 66.g6 ♗e3+ 67.♔b1 ♗d4 68.♖d5 ♗e3 69.♖a5 ♗d4 70.♖a6 ♗e3 71.♗f5 ♗d4 72.♖e6+ ♔f8 73.♖d6 ♗e5 74.♖d5 ♗f6 75.♗e4 ♔g7 76.♖d7+ ♔f8 77.♖f7+
Black resigned.

Grischuk obtained a sizable lead thanks to blunders by Caruana late on Day 2 and early on Day 3. He blundered a queen in one game, while he still had plenty of time, and checkmate in two in the other, giving away many points. Sometimes, to turn around an ugly score, some combination of luck and skill has to be involved, and Caruana got what he needed in the following scramble:

**Fabiano Caruana
Alexander Grischuk**
St. Louis 2017 (15)

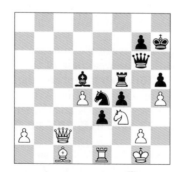

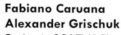
position after 41...♕g6

42.a4
At this point in the match, Grischuk was well ahead. In the diagrammed position, most moves win for Black, but in blitz it's important to finish off your opponent.
42...♘f2 43.♕e2 ♕g3 44.♖f1

44...♘h3+?! After 44...♘g4 White gets mated pretty soon. **45.♔h1 ♘f2+ 46.♔g1** Without increments, repeating moves only wastes time. **46...♗xf3 47.♕xf3 ♕xf3 48.gxf3 ♖a5?!** 48...♘d3 was winning. **49.♖e1 ♖xa4 50.♗xe3 fxe3 51.♖xe3**

Grischuk was working with less than 20 seconds, and Caruana smartly starts playing for the clock. His pawns don't matter, but he has to avoid the rook trade. **51...♘h3+ 52.♔g2 ♘f4+ 53.♔g3 ♖xd4 54.♖e5 ♔h6 55.♖f5 ♘g6 56.♖a5 ♖xh4 57.♖a6 ♖d4 58.♔f2 ♖f4 59.♔e3 ♖f6 60.♖a5 ♘h4 61.f4 ♘g6 62.♔f3 ♖xf4+ 63.♔e3 ♖g4 64.♔d2 ♖g5 65.♖a6**

Flag! A lucky break, after which Caruana got momentum.

Caruana won the next game and then the following one:

**Fabiano Caruana
Alexander Grischuk**
St. Louis 2017 (17)
Semi-Slav D42

1.c4 ♘f6 2.♘c3 c5 3.♘f3 e6 4.e3 ♘c6 5.d4 d5 6.cxd5 ♘xd5 7.♗d3 ♗e7 8.0-0 0-0 9.♗e4 ♘xc3!?
9...cxd4 10.exd4 ♗f6 11.♖e1 transposes to a very well-known position.
10.bxc3 ♕c7 11.♕c2 h6 12.♗h7+ ♔h8 13.♗d3 b6 14.e4

White has the centre, but Black is trying to counterattack. Pretty typical stuff for this pawn structure.
14...♗b7 15.♗e3 ♖ac8 16.♖ac1 ♖fd8 17.♕e2 ♕b8 18.♖fd1
Here is where the fun begins. Grischuk has a few reasonable alternatives, although the computer recommends getting the king out of h8 as soon as possible.

18...♗f6?
'Tempting' White to play e5. Well, Caruana doesn't need to be asked twice! Decisions like these aren't easy

Three-time Blitz World Champion Alexander Grischuk seemed to be in full control, but Fabiano Caruana showed great resilience on the final day and decided the match in his favour.

to make with a quick time-control. Pushing e5 is obviously extremely committal, but it has great attacking potential.
19.e5! ♗e7

20.♗xh6!
This is the big problem, and what Grischuk had overlooked. Now White gets a huge attack.
20...♘xd4!
Staying in the game was half the battle in many cases during the Showdown. Nakamura proved that no matter how bad his positions were, there were always possibilities to bounce back.
After 20...gxh6 21.♕e4 Black gets mated in a few moves.
21.♘xd4 gxh6

22.♕h5! Not letting up is key. If White retreats, Black will find himself with counterchances, and in blitz anything can happen. 22.♘b5 ♖g8 is messy. **22...♗g5 23.h4** White's only move.

23...♕xe5 And this is Black's only move. After 23...♗xc1 24.♖xc1

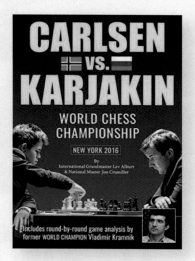
Black can't protect against the mating threats, for example: 24...♔g7 25.♘xe6+! fxe6 26.♕g6+ ♔f8 27.♕xh6+ ♔g8 28.♕xe6+ ♔f8 29.♕f5+ ♔e8 30.♕h5+ ♔f8 31.♕h8+ ♔f7 32.♕h7+ ♔f8 33.♗g6 ♖c7 34.♕h8+ ♔e7 35.♕f6+ ♔d7 36.♗f5+ ♔e8 37.e6, with mate coming up. It is not necessary to see this in a 10-minute game, but intuition should be enough to suggest that Black won't survive.

24.hxg5 ♕xg5 25.♕xg5 hxg5 26.♘f3

The smoke has cleared and White is up a piece. The pawn structures make his task easier, since the bishop already controls many squares on the queenside.

26...♗xf3?!

Even though this is objectively the best move, it makes no practical sense to allow the white bishop to dominate so freely.

27.gxf3 ♔g7 28.♗a6 ♖b8 29.♔g2 ♔f6 30.a4 ♖h8 31.♖h1 ♖xh1 32.♖xh1 ♖d8

The rest was easy, even with both players short on time.

33.♗b5 ♖d2 34.♖h8 ♖c2 35.c4 ♔e5 36.♖a8 f5 37.♖xa7 ♔f4 38.♖b7 e5 39.♖xb6 g4 40.fxg4 e4 41.♖f6 e3 42.♖xf5+ ♔xg4 43.♖f3 e2 44.♖e3 ♔f4 45.a5 ♖a2 46.a6 ♔g4 47.a7

Black resigned.

A tense match entering the last day. Caruana was two games behind (4 points). The day started like the rest of the match: Caruana scored two wins with his first two Whites, only for Grischuk to pounce back. However, in the end Caruana was the more resilient player. He won his last four Blacks to finish with a comfortable lead and took the match. This was a surprise to many, who had given three-time Blitz World Champion Grischuk a big edge in blitz, a format that Caruana isn't known for.

Blood on the clock

As far as the matches went, So-Dominguez was the most thrilling one, even though Day 1 was boring: three drawn Berlins and Dominguez winning the fourth game due to a blunder in a time-scramble. The true drama started with Day 2. Round 5 of the G/20 has made waves around the Internet, a few praising it as true entertainment and most bashing it as a return to caveman chess. So had 11 seconds to Dominguez's 7, and an extra pawn on the board. After that, all of the following happened: So stood up, Dominguez played with two hands, So played ♖e5, Dominguez captured that rook, which at some point returned to the h-file, Dominguez started laughing, So hesitated and despite his time edge he ended up flagging. The players tried to agree to a draw, but the arbiters pointed out So had already lost on time. The arbiters failed to intervene while all of this was happening, which prompted another players' meeting the next day.

Due to complaints by Wesley So's stepmother and manager Lotis Key and the obvious controversies that

True entertainment or a return to caveman chess? The clash between Wesley So and Leinier Dominguez was certainly a spectacle you don't see every day.

these time-controls brought, a system of instant replay was incorporated. The arbiters were instructed to be much more severe with calling out illegal moves, double-handed moves and similar situations. If a player wanted to appeal an arbiter decision, the arbiters would review the tape to see if the ruling stood or not. The truly amazing part is that not only was this never used, the arbiters never had to make a ruling throughout any of the G/10 or G/5 matches.

The Cuban had accumulated a strong lead halfway through the third day, and So at some point seemed dejected. However, he somehow pulled himself together, scoring three victories to pull back his 16-point deficit to a manageable 7. On the final day, Wesley So was simply on a rampage. He did not care about anything in the world except winning – his determination was fierce. So fierce, in fact, that he banged the clock loud enough for Carlsen to request that the organizers move this rambunctious match to the furthest board away from him, as he was being distracted. So fierce, indeed, that So literally bloodied his hands hitting the clock. The young Amer-

ican absolutely crushed the last day and turned around a seemingly irrepairable match with a full round to spare. Here is a fine blitz effort by So.

Leinier Dominguez
Wesley So
St. Louis 2017 (16)
Caro-Kann, Advance Variation

1.e4 c6 The Caro-Kann is not in Wesley So's main repertoire set, but it's nice to see him deviate from the Berlin Defence. Dominguez uses the current topical line against it.
2.d4 d5 3.e5 ♗f5 4.♘f3 e6 5.♗e2 ♘e7 6.c3

This set-up with an early c3 is how Topalov played against Nakamura on the first day.

6...♘d7 7.0-0 c5 8.dxc5!? ♘c6
8...♘xc5 is definitely the main line, as was seen in, for example, Caruana-Tari earlier this year.
9.b4
White holds on to the pawn on the queenside and lets go of the e5-pawn. The point is that Black's dark-squared bishop is rather restricted and White gets access to d4.
9...a5?!
So is in no hurry to regain the pawn, but this gives Dominguez time to reinforce the centre. Looking at the position for a couple of minutes, it is obvious that a5 is dubious, but a couple of minutes are very valuable!
10.♘d4 ♗g6 11.b5?!
11.f4 is the ambitious way to play, but it comes with some risk: 11...axb4 12.♘xc6 bxc6 13.cxb4 ♕b8 14.♗d2 ♗e7, although objectively White is simply much better.
11...♘cxe5

12.f4?!
This move looks strange. Leaving tactical weaknesses in a blitz game is a very dangerous thing to do, and So exploits it quickly.
On the other hand, 12.c6 bxc6 13.bxc6 ♘f6 14.♘a3!? is hard enough to assess in a normal game, and impossible in a blitz game.
12...♘c4 13.c6 bxc6 14.bxc6
14.♗xc4 dxc4 15.f5 would give White some initiative, but is still insanely complex. Black has resources to defend and White's structure is suspect.
14...♘f6 15.♕a4? The ghost of a discovered attack might make lesser

players 'defend' against c7+, but even in blitz, So is well aware that he won't need to.

15...♗c5! Suddenly the weakening of the a7-g1 diagonal is being felt.
16.♘a3 After 16.c7+ ♕d7 17.♕xd7+ ♔xd7 White simply loses his c7-pawn, and his development is sad.

♔xd7 is almost as bad as the game continuation.
17...♕d7 18.♕xd7+ ♔xd7 19.♘xc4

19...♘xc3! All White's pieces are hanging and So starts collecting material.
20.♘e5+ This doesn't help White at all, but it was difficult to recommend

Not your everyday blitz. Wesley So's determination was so fierce that he bloodied his hands on the clock.

16...♘e4! Playing with the initiative seems to come very naturally. During the Showdown, players found it easy to attack and create threats, but defending with the seconds ticking down is not so easy.
17.c7+
17.♗xc4 ♘xc3 18.c7+ ♕d7 19.♕xd7+

anything. Playing lightning fast, Black had also accrued a huge time advantage: almost five minutes!

20...♔xc7 21.♔h1 ♗xd4 22.♗f3 ♘e4 23.♗a3 ♘f2+ 24.♖xf2 ♗xa1 25.♖f1 ♗xe5 26.fxe5 ♔d7
White resigned.

On a different level

Which takes us to the fourth and final match, regarded by many as the main course, and for good reason. Magnus Carlsen isn't a player whose competitive spirit can be easily quenched. When he wins, he might think it was not by a large enough margin. If the margin is large, he might complain his chess wasn't the best. Watching Carlsen dominate this year's Paris and Leuven Rapid & Blitz events left no doubt that his intuition, skills, and whatever tool set you need to play blitz are ahead of anyone else's.

Ding Liren seemed like a worthy challenger: one of the select few that had already qualified to the Candidates', and a former number 1 in the FIDE blitz rating system (a system which, admittedly, is unbelievably flawed). The match did not seem to indicate that these two players were on the same level. Like the Americans, Carlsen was given a choice of opponents. His reasoning behind Ding Liren was that 'he is a very good player'.

The first day brought some thrills. The Chinese player had a huge advantage in the first G/30 game, only to let it slip. Carlsen won the fourth round with a beautiful subtlety.

Ding Liren
Magnus Carlsen
St. Louis 2017 (4)

position after 33.♖a1

33...♔f8 Black obviously has pressure, but making progress isn't easy. On the other hand, White doesn't have a lot of moves.

34.♖b2? And this is a mistake. White should have tried 34.♖c1. Carlsen spots his chance like a hawk.

34...♖c3! The rook leaves a3 and the a2-pawn is now too weak.

35.♖d2

35.♔d2 a3! is the beautiful point: 36.♔xc3 axb2 (36...♖c8+ is also winning) 37.♔xb2 ♗g4, and the d-pawn cannot be caught.

35...a3 36.♖b1 ♗c4

The computers might hold this, but in human practice this is just lost.

37.♖b4 ♖c1+ 38.♔f2 ♗xa2 39.♖a4 ♖c3! 40.♖xa2 ♖c2+ White resigned.

Day 2 was no better for Ding Liren: a bunch of draws and Carlsen scored three wins. Things kept getting worse and worse for the Chinese player. Though Ding Liren won the first game of G/10, Carlsen retaliated with four in a row. The match was mathematically over before the last round of the third day. Due to a silly FIDE rule which came to the spotlight following an incident involving Nigel Short and Hou Yifan in the Netherlands (Hoogeveen) last year, games are not

'Due to a silly FIDE rule, games are not rated once a match is mathematically won.'

rated once a match is mathematically won. For this reason, almost none of Nakamura's games and none of Carlsen's games in the last days counted for FIDE blitz rating. This was significant for Carlsen only, since the crushing score of 8½-3½ (everyone stopped using the weighted system by this point) would have catapulted Carlsen to over 3000.

Here is a typical game in the faster time-controls:

**NOTES BY
Peter Heine Nielsen**

**Magnus Carlsen
Ding Liren**
St. Louis 2017 (5)
Ruy Lopez, Morphy Defence

Games with quicker time-controls are obviously of varying quality, but precisely the lack of time to find the best defensive resources often has the effect that we see more clear-cut games in which the winner shows the best understanding of the basic strategy of an opening variation.

1.e4 e5 2.♘f3 ♘c6 3.♗b5 a6 4.♗a4 ♘f6 5.0-0 ♗e7 6.d3 b5 7.♗b3 d6 8.a3 0-0 9.♘c3

In such a long match, many openings can be tested, but here the players

enter a theoretical discussion of the line that was seen as many as four times in the previous World Championship match in New York, the difference being, however, that Magnus now has the white pieces.

9...♘a5

The main move, and what Magnus played twice against Karjakin in New York. 9...♗e6 and 9...♘b8 were also tested there, but the text-move is the preferred move for Black by quite a margin.

10.♗a2 ♗e6

11.b4 Again the main move. Karjakin first tried 11.d4, but was effectively neutralized after 11...♗xa2 12.♖xa2 ♖e8!?, which was a novelty at the time.

11...♗xa2

Ding again sticks to the main road. It would have been interesting if he had repeated Magnus' 'off-beat' choice of 11...♘c6, which netted him the important win in the third tiebreak game, which finally gave him the lead in the match. But we will have to wait for a next time before Magnus will reveal what idea he had prepared against it for White.

12.♖xa2

Here, Karjakin played the novelty 12.♘xa2 against Aronian in the Rapid part of St. Louis this summer, possibly revealing what surprise he was hoping to spring at the crucial

moment of the match, if Magnus had not deviated one move earlier.
12...♘c6 13.♗g5

13...♕d7 Ding shows his hand, and does not follow the more popular 13...♘d7, the latest trend being 14.♗d2 ♘f6 15.♖e1!?, which gave Maxime Vachier-Lagrave a promising position before it ended in a draw in the Palma de Mallorca FIDE Grand Prix only a week after the current game, showing how rapidly the theory develops in this line.

14.♗xf6 ♗xf6 15.♘d5 a5!?

A very interesting decision. 15...♗d8 has also been tried, but while obviously solid, it also looks passive. Black immediately attacks White's pawn structure and noteworthy enough does not fear the doubling of his pawns after 16.♘xf6+ gxf6.

16.c4 ♘e7

Necessary, since 16...axb4 17.cxb5 ♘e7 18.a4! is far better for White. Now Black essentially wins the battle for the a-file. But Magnus has his eyes elsewhere anyway:

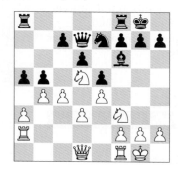

17.♖c2! ♘xd5

Also possible was 17...bxc4!?, essentially forcing White to finally take on f6, when, after 18.♘xf6+ gxf6 19.dxc4, White might still have a small edge in a position likely to be tested in the future.

18.cxd5 axb4 19.axb4 ♖a4 20.♕d2 ♖fa8 21.♖fc1 ♗d8

Everything proceeded logically. Black managed to double on the a-file and use his bishop to cover his only weakness on c7. In the meantime,

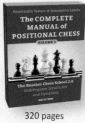

Magnus covered b4 and doubled on the c-file. The question remaining is: does Black have a safe fortress or will White be able to make progress?

22.h3 ♖a1 23.♖xa1 ♖xa1+ 24.♖c1 ♖a4 25.d4

25...exd4?

A strategic blunder, most likely because of a tactical oversight.
25...f6! was the critical move, keeping the position closed. Magnus would have to start regrouping, and 26.♘e1 looks like the first step. To me it looks like an unpleasant task for Black, and although the computers are not terribly pessimistic, it looks likely that Black will have to focus on an improvement on move 17 for future reference.

26.♘xd4 ♗f6 27.♘c6

White now threatens to attack the b5-pawn with his queen, and the obvious attempt to stop that contains a tactical flaw.

27...♕c8?? 28.e5! Winning immediately. Since 28...♗xe5 loses to the obvious fork on e7, Ding has no choice but the game continuation.

28...dxe5 29.d6! ♖a8

29...♕d7 would have allowed a more

beautiful finish: 30.dxc7?! ♕xc7 31.♘e7+ does win the queen and the game, but much more efficient is 30.♘e7+! ♗xe7 31.♖xc7, instantly winning, the basic point being 31...♕xd6 32.♖c8+!.

30.♘e7+ ♗xe7 31.dxe7

And while Black is technically a pawn up, there is no way to stop ♖d1, followed by ♕d8, as e.g. 31...♕e8 fails to 32.♖xc7. And so Ding resigned.

∎ ∎ ∎

Truly, Carlsen seemed to play on a different level, not just compared to Ding Liren but compared to any other participant. Though he made mistakes, he never blundered. He was never behind on the clock, and flagged Ding Liren every time he

had a chance by combining over-the-board pressure with extremely smart time management. This allowed him to save half points here and there, and they added up. Similar to Paris and Leuven, it seemed like he was playing classical chess and everyone else was playing blitz. It was shocking to see a player of Ding Liren's strength being so thoroughly zapped of his spirit. In the final games of the G/5, he would resign by looking at the board as if wondering what sins he had committed that the gods had put him through this punishment, and weakly extending his hand. Carlsen was always focused, cheerful. Like Teddy KGB and his Oreo cookies in *Rounders*, he picked up an easy tell for when he was deeply thinking: grabbing a couple of pawns and toying with them. After the display he would proceed with a series of moves which either solved all his problems or gave him the advantage. It was as though Ding Liren couldn't impact the game at all. To top it all off, Carlsen said in his interview: 'I am not 100% thrilled with the way things went today; he had so many chances!' This is true, but as Nakamura proved, chances are a far cry from results.

Let's round off with a sovereign display by the World Champion on Day 2 in the G/20 games.

Ding Liren
Magnus Carlsen
St. Louis 2017 (8)
English Opening, Four Knights

1.c4 ♞f6 2.♞c3 e5 3.♞f3 ♞c6 4.e3 ♝b4 5.♕c2

White is using some type of Reversed Sicilian, which is hard to find in top grandmaster chess. One of the good things about faster time-controls is that players are more willing to step out of their comfort zone. That doesn't always work out, though.

5...d6 6.♞d5 ♝a5 7.a3 ♞xd5! 8.cxd5 ♞e7 9.b4 ♝b6 10.♝c4 0-0 11.♝b2 ♝f5 12.d3 ♞g6

13.h4?! Ding Liren plays it in a risky way by pushing his h-pawn, which makes castling on the kingside more difficult but seems to put pressure on his opponent. A mere mortal might be scared of the advance, but Carlsen simply welcomes it.
13.0-0 ♞h4 14.♞xh4 ♕xh4 15.a4 a5 16.b5 seems to be to be a bit more

pleasant for Black, but the silicon monsters are convinced of equality.
13...h6 14.h5 ♞e7 15.♞d2 ♖c8!
Carlsen's understanding is completely on point. The break on c6 is not as strong immediately as it is with good preparation.

16.e4?! Too ambitious. The opening of the bishop on b6 cannot be underestimated. Interesting was 16.♕d1!? c6 (16...♕d7!?, keeping an eye on the kingside, might also be considered: 17.e4 ♝h7 18.g4 c6, with a black edge) 17.dxc6 ♞xc6 18.g4! (at this point, White should really try something like this) 18...♝e6 19.♝xe6 fxe6 20.♖c1. This position is still far from clear, but Black is to be preferred.
16...♝g4 17.d4
Ding Liren sacrifices a pawn, with the obvious idea to recapture it under favourable circumstances. After all, how can such a pawn on d4 survive?
17...exd4 18.f3?!
18.♕d3 immediately was better. White's king will suffer after f3.
18...♝d7 19.♕d3 c6!

Carlsen's timing is immaculate. White's position, almost out of the blue, is impossible to sustain. One

would think that with pieces like the bishop on d7 and the knight on c6, there must be a way to at least restrict the damage, but the truth is that White is totally lost.
20.dxc6 After 20.♝xd4 cxd5 21.exd5 ♝xd4 22.♕xd4 ♞f5 Black has a crushing attack, with moves like ...♖e8 and ...♞e3 coming.
20...♝xc6 20...♞xc6 was also good, but Carlsen's solution is clear-cut.
21.b5 ♝d7 22.0-0 d5 23.exd5 ♞f5 24.♞e4 ♞xd5 25.♝xd5 ♕xd5 26.♖ad1 ♖fd8

Black's up a pawn and the rest is trivial for the World Champion.
27.♖fe1 ♖c3! The rook is obviously taboo. White resigned.

A man full of ideas
The players expressed different opinions on the format, but no one had a major complaint about it. Somehow or another, almost no pieces went flying and no major controversies happened. It is as if real chess could be played in such a time-control, as opposed to a caveman flinging of the weighted wooden figures. This might scare many people who fear reverting the game to no increments or delays, especially those that prefer adjournments over rapid chess, but much of the spectator world was swayed by Carlsen's embrace of the challenge, even before he went on his rampage. There are currently no plans to host another major tournament without increments or delays, but Rex Sinquefield was very pleased with the four matches, and he is a man full of ideas. Don't be surprised if a new event pops up on the chess calendar! ∎

MAXIMize
your Tactics
with Maxim Notkin

Find the best move in the positions below

Solutions on page 93

1. White to move

2. White to move

3. White to move

4. White to move

5. Black to move

6. White to move

7. Black to move

8. White to move

9. White to move

More than the sum of its parts

Coaching a team is not merely a matter of fielding the strongest players. Before she turns to other matters of interest in our next issue, **JUDIT POLGAR** allows us another peek behind the scenes in a last column about her experiences as Hungary's team captain.

In most Olympiads that I participated in myself as a player, the classification was still determined by board points. But as the captain of the Hungarian team, I faced the relatively new system based on match points. Quite obviously, my main day-to-day concern was gathering the needed 2½ points (or more) to win the match, but I was also concerned about the well-being of the players. I had to make sure that they alternated colours, watch who was getting tired, and bear in mind the implications of previous individual results or the general compatibility against their likely opponents in the next round.

Keeping all this in mind, I decided to put Ferenc Berkes on Board 4 (above Csaba Balogh) at the 2015 European Team Championship in Reykjavik. I felt that if any of the players on the first three boards sat out, this would be the most functional team configuration. And at the 2016 Olympiad in Baku, where Peter Leko did not play and the young talent Benjamin Gledura was Board 5, I put Berkes on second board, as he is a solid player and I believed that Zoltan Almasi would be more effective as a puncher on Board 3.

In Reykjavik, the team strategy worked out well, since we conquered the bronze medals, and it could have worked in Baku as well, if it had not been for an unfortunate complication. In Leko's absence, Richard Rapport had to play on the first board, which for a creative player like him is always a double-edged affair. 'Ricsi' had married earlier that year, but shortly before the tournament the terrible news arrived that his father-in-law had died. These are not simple things to deal with and Rapport's play and result in Baku were his worst in many years.

The crucial moment in Reykjavik occurred in Round 7, in the match we won against Spain. Berkes played fantastically and should have won, but then he ruined everything and lost.

I know perfectly well how it feels in such cases, and after Berkes had resigned I stood next to his chair in complete silence. Words, even the kindest, can easily hurt after such a game... But then I realized that something was wrong with him. He turned very pale and looked as

if he was about to faint. I held his head and started talking to him. With a feeble voice Ferenc remembered that this was similar to another game from an earlier Olympiad, where we had been colleagues. I was heartbroken when I realized how much he had wished to contribute to the general success and that the pressure had simply been too great. I fetched him some sugar and he recovered very quickly, got up and went to his opponent to congratulate him. I let him go to the hotel only after assuring myself that Balogh would accompany him.

We had a long and difficult team meeting that night. Our next opponents were the Azeri team, a squad that was even stronger than before after Arkadij Naiditsch had joined them. Common sense suggested that after such a tough day Berkes should take a rest, but he assured me that he had recovered completely and that he wanted to play. I decided to keep him in the team and explained this to Balogh, who would be left out in this case. Although a bit sceptical, he understood my decision.

The next day, Berkes justified my trust by scoring an impressive technical win!

Ferenc Berkes
Eltaj Safarli
Reykjavik European Teams 2015

position after 47...a5

Our opponents were obviously surprised to see Berkes in the team after his collapse the previous day, but he played very confidently and treated the technical phase in style.

48.f6 Completely paralysing the bishop. White is practically a piece up. **48...♗f8 49.♗c1 a4 50.♗e3 ♘a5 51.♘d2 ♘c6 52.♗f3 ♘a5 53.g5 axb3 54.gxh6+ ♔h8 55.axb3 ♘xb3 56.♖b1 ♘a5 57.♖a1 ♘c6 58.♖a6 ♘d8 59.♖a8 b3 60.♖b8 ♔h7 61.♗g5+ ♔h8 62.♘xf7+ ♘xf7 63.♖xf8+ ♔h7 64.♖b8 ♖a7 65.♖xb3 ♖a4 66.♖c3 ♖a1 67.♖c1** Black resigned.

Quite a few new regulations have been introduced lately, most of them disturbing for the participants. Players are forbidden to wear watches and have their own pen, and captains are not allowed to have books with them. The most disturbing issues are that players can be scanned *during* the game for anti-

'The most disturbing issues are that players can be scanned *during* the game for anti-cheating purposes'

cheating purposes (especially taking into account that there is already a general scanning at the entrance before the game) or spend long and tiring hours after the game for the anti-doping checks. From our team, Gledura had the 'luck' of experiencing the first issue in Baku and Balogh the latter in Reykjavik. Furthermore, it is not easy to give a definitive evaluation of the 30-move rule, preventing players from agreeing to a short draw. But considering the pros and cons, I am positive about it, as it tends to improve the fighting level of the games.

During the two events in which I captained the Hungarian team, Balogh distinguished himself with his excellent preparation, his technique, patience, concentration, and the way he handled stress. He conquered the individual bronze medal on Board 5 in Reykjavik, but achieved his most crucial win in

Baku, in our match against the Netherlands in the penultimate round.

Csaba Balogh
Loek van Wely
Baku Olympiad 2016

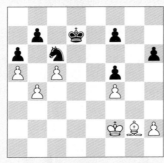

position after 48...♔xd7

White is obviously better, but winning is by no means trivial. Balogh managed to confuse and exhaust his opponent by moving his bishop to virtually all available squares, sometimes advancing his h-pawn until it reached h5. On move 89 he finally broke with b4-b5, and on move 113 his opponent resigned, sealing our win in the match.

position after 88...♔c8

89.b5 axb5+ 90.♗xb5 ♔c7 91.♔d4 ♔b8 92.a6 bxa6 93.♗xa6 ♔c7 94.♗b5 ♔b7 95.♔c4 ♔c7 96.♗a4 ♔b7 97.♗d1 ♔c7 98.♗f3 ♔d7 99.♔b5 ♔c7 100.c6 ♔d8

101.♔c5 ♘c8 102.♗g2 ♔e7 103. c7 ♔d7 104.♗b7 ♔xc7 105.♗xc8 ♔xc8 106.♔c6 ♔d8 107.♔d6 ♔e8 108.♔e6 ♔f8 109.♔xf6 ♔e8 110.♔g6 ♔e7 111.♔xh6 ♔f6 112.♔h7 ♔f7 113.h6 Black resigned.

When it turned out that Leko was not going to play in Baku, I decided to look for a replacement among the young Hungarian talents. My choice was Benjamin Gledura, who had been progressing a lot lately, scoring wins against former World Champions Karpov and Anand.

Benjamin's overall result justified my trust in him, but due to his lack of experience he ended the Olympiad on a sad note – for him and for the whole team.

Benjamin Gledura
Stelios Halkias
Baku Olympiad 2016

position after 23...♔g8

White is obviously better and Black, who was approaching severe time-trouble, has no counterplay at all. By this time two games were likely to end in draws, while Almasi had a difficult position. Gledura decided to change the course of the match with an unnecessary pawn sacrifice.

24.♖ae1 Gledura eventually got good compensation, but when Almasi managed to turn the tables and was clearly winning, our youngest player could not adopt himself to the new situation. He pushed too hard and lost. Instead of an honourable 6th place (especially if we think that Leko did not play and Rapport was out of shape), we finished only 15th...

Let's return to the 2015 European Team Championships in Reykjavik. One of my most aesthetically inspiring moments during my tenure as captain happened when I was standing next to Ferenc Berkes' board and the following position appeared in his game:

Anton Korobov
Ferenc Berkes
Reykjavik European Teams 2015

position after 33.♕b2

Black had outplayed his opponent in the middlegame and his minor pieces are stronger than the queen, especially with the white king in a delicate situation. After some thought Berkes played:

33...♖c3

This move yielded Black an advantage but unfortunately he failed to convert it.

While he was thinking, I calculated the following fantastic line: 33...♘cxe4+! 34.fxe4 ♘xe4+ 35.♔h3 (35.♔h4 ♗c8!, winning, or 35.♔f3 ♖b1!, and wins, are simpler) 35...♖c3+ 36.g3 ♘g5+ 37.♔h4.

37...♗c8!! (the key move in the whole sequence) 38.♕xc3 ♘f3+! 39.♕xf3 g5+ 40.♔h5 g6 mate.

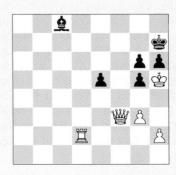

After the game Berkes told me that if he had found this combination, this would have been his most beautiful game ever.

With these reminiscences about three of the younger Hungarian talents I end my series about my experiences as team captain. But there is still a lot I would like to share with you as a NIC columnist, as you will see in the next issue! ■

1. Vidit-Areshchenko
Linares tt 2017

The rook is not the main driving force in the attack but just bait: **34.♖b8! f3+ 35.♔h1** Black resigned. Next comes 36.♕a1+, mating.

2. Zvjaginsev-Antipov
Sochi 2017

18.♘d5! ♕xd5 19.♕xd5+ ♘xd5 20.♖xe8+ ♔f7 21.♖ae1! b5 If 21...♘xf4 22.♖1e7 mates. **22.♗d6 ♗b7 23.♖8e7+** Black resigned.

3. Wang Hao-Sengupta
World Cup, Tbilisi 2017

The bishop isn't safe on h7: **32.h5 ♗h7 33.♖d8+! ♘xd8 34.♖xd8+ ♔e7 35.♖h8** and White converted his material advantage.

4. Arizmendi-Smirnov
Barcelona 2017

24.♕b5+ An essential check to begin the queen hunt, which is all about pins and forks. **24...♔f7 25.♖xe4! ♕xe4 26.♘g5+! ♗xg5 27.♗xd5+** Black resigned.

5. Shanava-Matsenko
Turkey tt 2017

What to do about Black's nasty mating threat? **47...♘g6! 48.♖xg6 ♕f2+ 49.♖g2 ♕xg2+!** After 50.♔xg2 d2 a new queen is born. White resigned.

6. Perunovic-Romanishin
Biel 2017

30.♘b4! ♕a8 30...♕xd1+ 31.♖xd1 ♗xd1 32.♘d5 is a hopeless ending. **31.♘d5! ♗xd1 32.♘f6! c4** Or 32...♗f3 33.♘xh7+ ♔g8 34.♘f6+ and 35.♖e8+. **33.♘xh7+ ♔g8 34.♘f6+ ♔h8 35.♖xd1** And White won.

7. Wallace-Goganov
Biel 2017

29...♘exf5! 30.exf5 ♗g2! 31.♕xg2 If 31.♕h4(h6), 31...♘xf5 traps the queen. **31...♖xg2+ 32.♔xg2 ♘xf5 33.♖g3** The rook cannot be saved: on 33.♖c3 ♘g6+ 34.♔f2 ♖g8 wins. **33...♘xg3 34.hxg3 d5** and Black duly won.

8. Petrosian-Panjwani
Philadelphia 2017

33.♘f7! 33.♕xd8?? f3+ 34.♔g1 ♕d1+ 35.♔h2 ♕f1. **33...f3+** If 33...♖e8 34.♕xd7 ♕e4+ 35.f3 the ♔ walks to g4. **34.♔h2 ♕f5** If 34...♕f1 35.♖xh6+ gxh6 36.♘g5+ mates. But now: **35.♖xh6+! gxh6 36.♘d6+** Black resigned.

9. Morozov-Prince
Paleochora 2017

33.♖d7! ♔xe5 After 33...♖xd7 34.♕h8+ ♔g7 35.♘xd7+ Black is totally lost. **34.♕h8+! ♔f4 35.g3+ ♔f3 36.♗d1+ ♔f2** Or 36...♔e3 37.♕c3+ mating. **37.♕b2+ ♔e1 38.♕e2** Mate.

15 minutes of chess

What do you look for when you are seriously short of time and don't want to interrupt your chess training? Absorbed by long days at work, our reviewer **MATTHEW SADLER** was happy to receive more than one book with series of instructive positions.

The past few months have seen me in constant time trouble as I've relocated to the UK while struggling to keep a big IT project limping along. From the chess point of view, I'm always a little nervous about such busy periods in my life as even short interruptions in my chess training have a severe effect on me. A couple of weeks without any chess as an amateur feels like the equivalent of a 3-months' break as a professional. I don't understand why, but it feels as if life and work are continually eating away greedily at my brain capacity, and if I don't defend myself then they will gobble up the little space I had left over for chess too. And getting it back is 100 times harder than giving it away.

So, my miracle solution is a minimum of 15 minutes' chess every day. Doesn't sound like much, but as any working person will tell you, those 15 minutes can get squeezed out very easily during a hectic period. Books can help you in this, but you obviously need books that cater to someone with a short attention span! From that point of view, I have

mostly been happy with the books that have landed on my doorstep this past month. In particular, I was very keen on books that dealt with series of instructive positions. I got into the rhythm of reading them during breakfast, making a note in my phone of positions that particularly appealed to me, and even setting up some of those on any chessboards I had lying around the house. My theory was that I would absorb some of the lessons from those positions better if I noticed the positions from time to time and thought 'Oh yes, ...♗c5!'. No idea if it worked, but at least I easily made my daily 15 minutes!

I'd had *The Complete Manual of Positional Chess* (Volume 1 – Opening and Middlegame, and Volume 2 – Middlegame Structures and Dynamics) lying around the house for a few months before getting into them. The books are written by two very strong Russian grandmasters and coaches – Konstantin Sakaev and Konstantin Landa – and are billed as 'probably the most thorough grounding in the history of teaching chess'. I dipped a little bit into Volume

1 a while back, and I wasn't sure what the fuss was all about. My first quick way of assessing such books is to see how many of the selected positions are unfamiliar to me. The more examples unknown to me, the more original a book is likely to be. From that point of view, Volume 1 is a little disappointing, as a great many familiar classics are used to illustrate the 30 themes (each assigned a chapter). On second reading, I was inclined to be much milder – the book probably fitted my mood and needs much better than before – but the wow-factor (which the blurb makes you expect) was not really there: it's simply a professional, solid effort.

I found Volume 2 much more interesting however: this is a very good book. This volume covers 58 themes such as 'The solidity of the king's cover', 'The attack with the rook's pawn', 'Intermediate moves', 'Unstable position of pieces' or 'X-rays'. Of the 373 positions in total, I noted down 79 which I would like to remember something about, which is a pretty good total considering that this book is probably aimed at players around 2000-2100 or coaches wishing to give younger players a thorough grounding in the basics. I'll just give you an impression of some of the positions that I noted down.

Jones-Pantsulaia
Warsaw 2013
position after 55.♕e1

Taken from Chapter 47 – Exploiting Diagonals. Sakaev and Landa point out the chance that Black missed in the game: **55...♖e5** Stunning! Those are the moves that you just want to pop into your head without thinking! In the game 55...♔h8 56.♘f6 ♕xe1 57.♗xe1 ♖d8 58.♖c7 ♗d3 led to a draw in 85 moves.

56.♗xe5 ♗xe5+ 57.♔g3
57.♔g2 ♕g4+ 58.♘g3 ♗b7+.
57...♕a2+ 58.♔h3 ♗b7

He can only avoid mate on g2 with the help of the queen, but it is tied to the defence of the knight.

59.♕f1 59.♕e2 ♕e6+ 60.♔h2 ♗xg3+. **59...♕e6+ 60.♔h2 ♗xg3+ 61.♔xg3 ♕g4+ 62.♔f2 ♕f4+ 63.♔e2 ♗a6+** Winning.

The following position is taken from Chapter 11 – Connected Pawns. Again a position where you want to be able to make the right move almost without thinking!

Mamedyarov-Balogh
Ningbo 2011
position after 18.♖a1

The two advanced connected pawns, supported by the bishop, are fully worth a piece, and so there followed:
18...♘xb2 If he retreats with

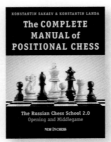

The Complete Manual of Positional Chess Volume 1 by Konstantin Sakaev & Konstantin Landa, New in Chess, 2016
★★★☆☆

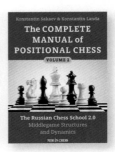

The Complete Manual of Positional Chess Volume 2 by Konstantin Sakaev & Konstantin Landa, New in Chess, 2017
★★★★☆

18...♘b6, then after 19.♘xa5 ♕d7 20.♘b3, it is not so simple to play ...c6-c5, and White's position is slightly preferable.

19.♕xb2 a4 20.♘bd2 c5 The fact that Black has been able to play ...c6-c5, opening up his light-squared bishop and exerting pressure on the centre, was undoubtedly part of what persuaded him to play the sacrifice.

21.♗e4 By exchanging light-squared bishops, White reduces the attacking potential of the black pieces, but the same pawns are very strong all same and only need to be well-supported

21...♕b8 An excellent way to increase the pressure on the queenside

'Stunning! Those are the moves that you just want to pop into your head without thinking!'

was to include another fighting unit – the pawn on e6. The strongest move is the surprising 21...♗d5. Sooner or later, the exchange of bishops on d5 is unavoidable and Black's idea is to take back on d5 with the pawn. In this case he limits the activity of the ♘d2. In addition, White must himself take on c5, because of the threat of ...c5-c4. Play could then proceed roughly as follows: 22.♖fc1 a3 23.♕b1 ♖c8 24.♗xd5 exd5 25.dxc5 ♖xc5 26.♕d3 ♖xc1+ 27.♖xc1 ♕d7 and Black has a lasting initiative. The game continued:
22.♗xb7 ♕xb7 23.♘c4 b3 24.♘d6 ♕b4 25.dxc5 ♕xc5 26.♕d4 ♕xd4 27.♘xd4 b2 28.♖a2 ♖fb8 29.♖b1 a3 and was eventually drawn!

■ ■ ■

A couple of interesting newcomers to the publishing scene are livening up my reviewing activities. Elk and Ruby is mining a fascinating seam of Russian chess life and literature while Thinkers Publishing have already brought out a number of original titles that would definitely have been on my 'work through this and improve' list as a professional. A good example of this is *Together with Morozevich* by the Russian Grandmaster Alexey Kuzmin. He embarked on a career as a coach after ending his active playing career in 2004 and was Alexander Morozevich's second from 2006 to 2015. The format of the

first two chapters is unique to my knowledge. Kuzmin starts with a – inevitably for Morozevich – totally lunatic position in the middlegame and then sets 9 (difficult) test positions on the first position (from Morozevich-Vachier-Lagrave, Biel 2009)

Together with Morozevich by Alexey Kuzmin, Thinkers Publishing, 2017
★★★☆☆

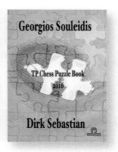

TP Chess Puzzle Book by Dirk Sebastian & Georgios Souleidis Thinkers Publishing, 2017
★★★☆☆

and Georgios Souleidis. The little twist to this puzzle book is the organisation of the material, which is anything but standard. There are chapters dedicated to young players (Anna Muzychuk and Jeffery Xiong), chapters dedicated to openings (the Benko Gambit, the Berlin), structures (IQP's, passed pawns) and specific sacrifices (♗xh6). It's all entertaining, and quite different from the normal pins and forks! My only quibble – probably inherent to the approach of grouping puzzles by such themes – is that the difficulty and type of solution required varies quite significantly within a chapter. For example, you get an easy win followed by a more difficult puzzle in which the end result is an initiative. That can stop you getting into a nice flow and solving rhythm. Personally, I'm

and no less than 26 equally difficult test positions on Grischuk-Morozevich, Russia 2004.

The other six chapters are more traditional in the sense that they first set a series of puzzles and then present the answers, although Chapter 4 does have 6 separate puzzles on the same game Kasparov-Morozevich, Bosnia 2000.

My thoughts about this book are as confused as Morozevich's positions! First of all, let's be clear: the material in this book is absolutely stunning. I can't imagine how many hours of work and creativity have been poured into this book, and it's a privilege to be able to see it. However... my goodness, what strength do you have to make good use of this book? Take the

first chapter. If you sneak a look ahead at the analysis, then the first chapter is useless as a training exercise – which is a real shame of course – so in fact you have to solve nine difficult test positions before you're allowed some fun! I did that – rather well in fact if you'll allow me some boasting – but I must have spent some 4-5 hours in total doing so (now you know why I get so irritated when people ask me

'My goodness, what strength do you have to be to make good use of this book?'

whether I read the books I review ☺). If it takes me that long, then I think it will be a huge undertaking for anyone below IM level. As for the second chapter, I worked my way through the first 7 tests, but with 19 more to go, even this lunatic amateur ran out of time, willpower and coffee beans. The sad thing is, I don't even feel I can share any of the solutions I found with you, because that would ruin it for anyone who wants to work seriously through the book!

I'm going to give the book 3 stars, with the remark that giving a star rating to this book is as useful as assessing a Morozevich middlegame as 0.00. It's in a class of its own, but I would only recommend getting this book if you are prepared to do some serious training!

■ ■ ■

A slightly easier offering from Thinkers Publishing is the *TP Chess Puzzle Book* by IMs Dirk Sebastian

also always reluctant to start solving puzzles that end in a 'slightly better for Black' evaluation. I can never convince myself that I'll end up agreeing with the correct solution! I think I'll give it a good 3 stars and keep on ploughing through them. One position that gave me a giggle when I saw it was this one:

NguyenThi Mai Hung-Lanchava
Baku Olympiad 2016
position after 39.♕xa5

Here Black repeated moves with checks on e1 and e5, but she had a very nice way of transforming a positional disadvantage in her position into an advantage.

39...♛e5+ 40.♚h1 c5

A sweet little move, exploiting the fact that White cannot take en passant. I wasn't 100% sure that we were really talking about a clear advantage as claimed in the puzzle, but Black has definitely improved her position substantially.

■ ■ ■

The last book for this month's reviews is *Mastering Complex Endgames* by Adrian Mikhalchishin & Oleg Stetsko. Mikhalchishin as an author always puts me into a bit of a quandary. I think he does a fantastic job of selecting instructive material for his DVD's and books, but this is normally accompanied by inexplicable carelessness in the execution. I previously reviewed one of his (very good) instructional DVD's which was rife with tactical errors. I don't think this is true in this case, but there are an astonishing number of typo's. Counting errors such as wrong moves in variations (...♘xf4 instead of ...♘xb4), missing moves, references to White instead of Black, I counted 20 in the first 300 pages without even making a particular effort. It's a real shame, because it's enough to put me off and detracts from what is a really excellent book! The book examines all sorts of endgames that are hard to categorise and thus rarely make it into standard ending manuals. The chapter I'm studying at the moment on rook against two minor pieces is an excellent case in point. As I said, the quality

Mastering Complex Endgames by Adrian Mikhalchishin & Oleg Stetsko, Thinkers Publishing, 2017
★★★★☆

of the material selected is superb, the comments sometimes a little carelessly formulated but often extremely instructive. I'm going to give it 4 stars, which essentially is 5 minus 1 – if I'd been spared the irritation of the typo's I think it would have squeaked a 5!

I'll just leave you with a little taste of the type of content in the book. For a lot of the games in this book – many taken from very recent practice – I was vaguely aware of them in the sense of 'Oh yes, Aronian won', but without having noticed them as special in any way. It's very gratifying therefore when an author can broaden your horizon and show you how good a game really was!

Aronian-Jakovenko
Khanty-Mansiysk Olympiad 2010
position after 20...♝e7

In spite of his worse pawn structure, Black's position looks quite reliable. Nevertheless, White can fight for an advantage by creating a weak pawn on c6.

21.♖a1 White wants to advance his a-pawn to a6 in order to remove the support of c6.

21...♘d7 22.a5 ♖a7 23.a6 bxa6 24.♖xa6 ♖xa6 25.♝xa6 ♖b8 26.♖c1

After exchanging a pair of rooks, the position assumes a technical character as Black is tied to the passive defence of his weak pawn on c6.

26...♖b6 27.♝e2 ♝f8 28.♚f1 A typical method of play in this kind of position. As Black cannot display any activity, White improves the position of his king and moves him to the centre of events. **28...g6 29.♚e1 ♚g7 30.♚d1 ♝e7 31.f4**

This one went on to my chessboard to be admired for a few days! A crucial move! White not only radically prevents ...e6-e5, but he also frees the f2-square in order to bring his knight to the ideal square d3, from where it will attack b4 and also control e5 and c5.

31...♚f8 32.♝f3 ♖a6 33.♘f2 c5 34.♘d3 ♖a5 35.♚e2 ♚g7 36.♖c2 ♝f8 37.♝c6 ♘b8 38.♝e8
Lovely! Now Black cannot avoid the loss of material.

38...♘a6 39.♝e5 cxd4 40.exd4 g5 41.♝xf7 ♖xe5+ 42.fxe5 ♚xf7 43.♖c6 ♘b8 44.♖c7+ ♝e7 45.b3 ♘a6 46.♖b7 1-0.

Wonderful play from Aronian! Thank you Mikhalchishin for pointing it out! Despite everything, highly recommended! ∎

Hans Ree

Recently, the Dutch historian Rob van Vuurde published *Adoe toean blanda, u staat schaakmat!,* a book about chess life in the period of Dutch colonial rule in Indonesia. For **HANS REE** it evoked fond memories of his own visit to the country.

The journey of a lifetime

I remember a review of one of my books that said (I quote from painful memory): 'Not many people will read this book, but to those who do, it will provide great pleasure.' Friendly enough, but not providing great pleasure to me. Not that I would have preferred the opposite, though.

The book *Adoe toean blanda, u staat schaakmat!,* a labour of love by the Dutch historian Rob van Vuurde, will probably find a limited readership. It is in Dutch, and it is about the history of chess in Indonesia during the period when it was not yet Indonesia, but a Dutch colony, 'Nederlands-Indië' or as the Dutch called it affectionately, 'our Indië'. For the general Dutch public, this period has almost slipped out of mind.

Though the book is mainly devoted to chess events that were organized within the NISB, the Dutch East Indies Chess Federation, it contains a lot of topics of general interest, not only for

chess players, but also for those who are interested in the history of the Dutch colonial era. I have belonged to the latter group since the time I played a tournament in Jakarta and gave a simul tour in cities on Java and Bali, in 1986.

The title of the book, half Indonesian and half Dutch, means 'Alas Dutch sir, you are checkmated.' It hints at the end of Dutch rule.

In 1945, a nationalist movement that had gained strength during the Japanese occupation declared independence for the erstwhile Dutch colony. The Dutch government resisted and started a war, that they euphemistically called a police intervention. It cost at least 100,000 Indonesian lives.

In 1949, a peace agreement was signed and Indonesia was born. Many Dutch colonists returned to the Netherlands, but a substantial number of them stayed. Then, around 1958, most of these left also, because of a sharpening conflict between the Netherlands and Indonesia over the area of Papua New Guinea (Irian Jaya) that the Dutch had kept out of the 1949 agreement to throw a bone to the Dutch groups that had campaigned with the slogan 'Indië lost, calamity born'. In Dutch it rhymes.

Paradise Lost

To the Dutch who had lived in Indonesia and gone back, it was a lost paradise. Most of them were no fools and were thoroughly aware that it was paradise, not only because of its breath-taking beauty of nature, but also because of the political situation, which made the Europeans masters. It was not a paradise for everyone.

Van Vuurde gives some statistics: around 1930, Indonesia (to use the anachronistic term) had a population of about 60 million, of which about 1.25 million were Chinese and about 250,000 were 'European', most of them Dutch. So the Dutch ruling class constituted less than half a percent of the general population, and the attitude of the government towards the vast majority oscillated between a benevolent paternalism and repression, depending on the political circumstances.

Until early in the 20th century, the Chinese had to live in their own city districts and had to apply for a pass whenever they wanted to leave the area. In public they had to dress in traditional Chinese costumes and were forced to wear the often hated Chinese queue.

According to Van Vuurde, several historians have maintained that around the 1930s, in response to the increasing nationalism , the authorities had turned the Dutch Indies into a police state. Press freedom was restricted and some organizations were forcibly dissolved. Nationalist leaders like Sukarno, Hatta and Sjahrir were arrested and interned in faraway concentration camps. I have always been amazed by the forgiveness that these leaders showed towards the Dutch after they had become the leaders of the new Indonesia.

I gained the impression from Van Vuurde's book that the NISB, an almost completely white organization, was never averse to involving the other ethnic groups, but as so often with well-meaning initiatives of white colonials, it was probably too little too late. Van Vuurde writes: 'Until the end, the NISB remained a predominantly European bulwark in a rapidly emancipating indigenous chess world. It was one of the reasons that the federation was slowly marginalized in the Dutch Indies chess world, groping for a way to survive.'

Another Kostic analysis room

In 1924, the Dutch writer Louis Couperus wrote about a visit to the Karo heights on the island Sumatra where the Bataks lived, famous in the chess world since 1904, when the German author Armin von Oefele wrote his book *Das Schachspiel der Bataker*.

Couperus saw a few immense stone chess pieces, the remnants of a set with which princes had played a game that lasted a year and was played on the high plains. At every move the immense pieces were carried by slaves; at stake were 12 slaves.

This may have been a fairy tale, but to all accounts the Bataks were very passionate players, and when European champions like the Yugoslav globetrotter Boris Kostic, Max Euwe and Alexander Alekhine toured the Dutch Indies, games against the best Batak players were on the programme. In his Dutch book '*Meneer*' *Caïssa*, written in collaboration with the journalist Bob Spaak, Euwe devotes a chapter to his games against the Batak players.

I was amused to read in Van Vuurde's book that during a blindfold simul by Kostic, who visited in 1925, people grew suspicious when the master retired to the toilet so often. Kostic toured all continents and perhaps had his special analysis rooms everywhere.

On August 1st, 1930, Max Euwe and his wife Caro boarded the ship Baloeran in Marseille to arrive in Sumatra on August 19th. Members of the chess club of Medan came to greet him and told him that the announcement of his visit had already increased their club's membership from 9 to 40.

Contrary to Kostic, Euwe made himself very popular. After his simul opponents

had consulted with others, moved the pieces in analysis and sometimes even tried to change the position, he declared that such irregularities were just a sign of an exaggerated respect for the visiting master. To the correspondent of the Dutch newspaper *De Telegraaf* he said, before boarding the Johan van Oldenbarnevelt for Genova on October 1st, that the trip had been the journey of a lifetime, an unforgettable experience which he would cherish for the rest of his life.

Your bag is a grandmaster!

Not that I want to compare myself with the great Max Euwe, but so it would prove to be for me.

In the summer of 1986, the Indonesian IM and chess official Max Wotulo came to the OHRA tournament in

'Euwe declared that such irregularities were just a sign of an exaggerated respect for the visiting master.'

Amsterdam to invite some players to participate in a tournament in Jakarta a few months later. I was among the lucky ones, but I had promised my wife that we would have a long holiday in that period. 'What better holiday for her than a trip to Indonesia?' said Wotulo. He was right.

The tournament would be won by the Yugoslav grandmaster Petar Popovic and the Indonesian IM Ardiansyah. I finished on a decent fifth place. Halfway the event, Wotulo came to pay me my appearance fee. A bit surprised, I said that in a telex he had promised me twice that amount. 'Oh no, that can't be right', he said. I produced the telex. Wotulo looked at it and with a friendly smile said: 'Yes, you're right, that was our mistake' and put the telex into his pocket.

Bad luck, I thought. But at the closing ceremony things were gloriously made right when the president of the Indonesian chess federation,

Mochtar Kusumaatmadja, who spoke a fluent formal Dutch, invited me for a tour of simuls in cities on Java and Bali with all expenses paid for me and my wife.

This was wonderful, because the month of touring we had envisaged might have become boring. Much better to have a job to do and talk to people on a basis of shared interests.

On my trip I saw the breath-taking natural beauty that had made so many Dutch colonists and visitors speak of paradise. I saw that chess was played on street corners, and when I was challenged to a game in Yogyakarta, I introduced myself as a grandmaster, showing a bag of the Jakarta GM tournament. I was deservedly ridiculed: 'Your bag is a grandmaster!'

I was embarrassed to see the bicycle taxis carrying whole Indonesian families with luggage, whereas they could hardly carry one big Dutchman.

I also felt a bit uneasy when I read in a newspaper that the Dutch foreign minister Hans van den Broek had said during a visit of a delegation of the European Union that he would speak with his esteemed colleague Mochtar Kusumaatmadja – not only the Indonesian Foreign Minister but also the President of its chess federation – about violations of human rights in Indonesia.

Good work by our minister, but what a pity that the Dutch had only embraced the concept of human rights after they had left the country and not while they were ruling it.

I made friends with the Chinese chess organizers on Bali, who seemed to be humorous cynics, more European than Asian. And all in all, it was, as Euwe had said, the journey of a lifetime, never to be forgotten. ■

Jan Timman

A Family Festival

A battle of generations and 'Jorden van Foreest's last chance' were the main attractions at the annual festival in Hoogeveen. But **JAN TIMMAN** also kept an eye on the games of 10-year-old Machteld van Foreest, perhaps the most talented scion of the Van Foreest dynasty.

For the fourth time, two interesting matches took place in Hoogeveen in the Netherlands, instead of the four-player double round-robin that used to be held here for many years as the main attraction of the annual chess festival. The idea to switch to matches was the brainchild of tournament director Loek van Wely, who invariably manages to invite four grandmasters that capture people's imagination. Last year's main match was a clash between the sexes – Nigel Short-Hou Yifan. This year the theme was a clash between generations, Vasily Ivanchuk being 30 years older than Wei Yi. In the early 1990s, Ivanchuk was seen as the big promise, the crown prince that might go on to succeed Kasparov, which he never did. Wei Yi, on the other hand, still has all the time in the world to make his dreams come true. More and more Internet reports are predicting that in the near future the world title will be in Chinese hands. This seems a slight exaggeration, but the Chinese team's successes have been striking. In addition, a Chinese player, Ding Liren, has qualified for the Candidates Tournament for the first time.

The second match was about 'Jorden van Foreest against the Rest of the World' again. In previous years, he had played against me and Ivan Sokolov, and now he would square up to Adhiban Baskaran, who had drawn attention to himself in Wijk aan Zee earlier this year with an excellent shared third place. During the opening ceremony, Van Wely said that this was going to be Jorden's last chance: he had lost against Sokolov and me, and this time he would finally have to win... Very unusual words for a tournament director, but no one seemed surprised, because we all know that Loek is not your average tournament director. His speeches in the opening and closing ceremonies tend to have been conceived mainly in order to entertain; they contain more witticisms than information.

Ivanchuk-Wei Yi

The main match turned out to be the less interesting one. The reason? Ivanchuk, although generally a very interesting player with his own original ideas, sometimes seems to lack inspiration and resorts to playing rather flat classical chess. As a result, the first two games ended in pretty lame draws. In the third game, however, something incredible happened.

Vassily Ivanchuk
Wei Yi
Hoogeveen 2017 (match-3)

position after 13...♖fe8

14.♔f2 This move gives you a glimpse of 'Planet Ivanchuk'. It's an uncommon way to develop one's king, and there was nothing against the normal developing move 14.♗e2, followed by castling kingside. The text turns out to have a psychological effect, because it causes Wei Yi to start looking for ideas to harass the white king.
14...♖ac8 The alternative was 14...♖e6, intending to meet 15.♗e2 with 15...b5. After 16.♖hc1 ♘b6 White has to go 17.♕d1!, withdrawing his queen to protect the knight. The position is dynamically balanced. With the text, Black is aiming to get the c-file opened.
15.♗e2 c5 16.dxc5 ♖xc5 17.♖hc1

The critical position.

17...g5 The start of an incorrect combination. If Black had wanted to sacrifice a rook, he should have played 17...♖xe3! at once, with the magnificent point that White will be mated after 18.♔xe3 d4+ 19.♔xd4 ♖c4+!! and the black queen will deliver the mate from c5 or e5 – a study-like combination. In order to neutralize the black attack, White would be forced to insert 18.♗xf6, and after 18...♖xe2+ 19.♔xe2 ♕a6+ 20.♔d1 ♖b5!, followed by a recapture on f6, Black would have sufficient compensation for the exchange.

18.♗g3

A high-spirited Vassily Ivanchuk admires an artist's impression of his match against Wei Yi after he has beaten his young opponent in two 10-minute tiebreak games.

18...♖xe3? In these circumstances, the rook sac won't work, since White controls the crucial e5-square.

19.♔xe3 d4+ 20.♔xd4

Unbelievable but true. It looks like a game of 'King of the Hill' (in this chess variant, the idea – besides mating the enemy king – is to get your king to one of the four central squares). The white king, surrounded by enemy pieces, turns out to be untouchable.

20...♖e5 Other moves also leave Black empty-handed.

21.♗d3 21.♗f1 would have won as well. **21...♗e6 22.♕xb7 ♔g7 23.♘e4 ♘d5 24.♗xe5+ ♘xe5 25.♖c5** Black resigned.

'Loek van Wely's speeches tend to have been conceived mainly in order to entertain; they contain more witticisms than information.'

The next two games were drawn again, which meant that Wei Yi had to try and win his last game as White. Ivanchuk opted for the Sicilian in what you could call a sporting gesture; he refused to duck behind a solid opening system like the Berlin Wall.

Wei Yi
Vassily Ivanchuk
Hoogeveen 2017 (match-6)
Sicilian Defence, Taimanov Variation

1.e4 c5 2.♘f3 e6 3.d4 cxd4 4.♘xd4 ♘c6 5.♘c3 a6 6.♘xc6 bxc6 7.♗d3 ♕c7
The most common move is the immediate 7...d5, but the text is also well-known, mainly from an old game between Spassky and Petrosian.

8.0-0 ♘f6 9.♕e2 d5 10.♗g5
The sharpest approach. The alternative is 10.b3, as in Bok-Artemiev, Tbilisi World Cup 2017.

10...♗b7 11.f4
Remarkably enough, this very position arose in Kollars-Gritsak in the Hoogeveen Open on the same day.

11...h6
Spassky-Petrosian, Palma de Mallorca 1969, saw 11...♗e7 12.e5 ♘d7 13.♗xe7 ♔xe7 14.♘a4 c5 15.c4

d4!, and Black had solved his opening problems. But it is extremely risky to keep your king in the middle in a sharp Sicilian. Petrosian took the risk, but things could have ended badly for him if Spassky had launched a sharper attack.

Kollars went for a plan that was more dangerous for Black: 14.♖ae1 (instead of 14.♘a4) 14...g6 15.♘d1. White is going to take his knight to e3 and then aim for f4-f5, which means he is going to sacrifice a piece – something that Black can do surprisingly little about.

12.♗h4 ♗e7

This was what Ivanchuk had intended. He was probably planning to meet 13.e5 with 13...♘e4. This is not entirely enough for equality, because White can play 14.♗xe7

♘xc3 15.♕g4! ♕xe7 16.♕xg7 before recapturing on c3. Wei Yi probably saw too many drawing tendencies here, because he decides on a different approach.

13.♗g3 Keeping all prospects in the position. **13...0-0** Very careless. Black should not have castled yet. A preventive move like 13...♘d7 would have been better, since it would have allowed him to meet 14.f5 with 14...e5. **14.e5 ♘e8 15.f5** Of course. **15... exf5 16.♗xf5 ♕b6+ 17.♔h1 g6**

18.♗d7!
This is Black's problem. The white bishop is hampering the coordination in the enemy camp. The advance of the e-pawn can no longer be prevented.

18...♖d8 19.e6 f5 20.♕d2 ♔h7 21.♗f2 ♕a5 22.♗e3

22...h5 Afterwards, Wei Yi indicated 22...♘f6, to eliminate the encroaching bishop, as better, but even then White retains an advantage after 23.♗xh6 ♘xd7 24.exd7 ♖f7 25.♖f3!. The black king remains exposed.

23.♕f2 c5 24.♕f4 With little moves, White forces his opponent to steadily weaken his position, after which the attack will play itself.

24...g5 25.♕f3 g4 26.♕f4 ♖f6

The match between Adhiban Baskaran and Jorden van Foreest was also decided in extra time. The young Dutchman prevailed, 2-0.

27.♗xe8 ♖xe8 28.♕g5 ♖ef8
29.♕xh5+ ♔g7 30.♕g5+ ♔h8
31.♕h5+ ♔g7 32.♗g5 d4
33.♗xf6+ ♖xf6 34.♖xf5
Black resigned.

Later that afternoon, two 10-minute tiebreaks were played, both of which Ivanchuk won. The next day, he played a number of draughts games against the Dutch top player Jan Groenendijk that didn't go so well for him. Afterwards, both Wei Yi and Ivanchuk flew to China to play in the league there.

Adhiban-Van Foreest

In the first game of the other match, Van Foreest lost a pawn in the early middlegame. After that he dug in and managed to scrape a draw.

Adhiban Baskaran
Jorden van Foreest
Hoogeveen 2017 (match-1)

position after 26...♗a2

If Adhiban had known what was coming, he would undoubtedly have played 27.♖b4 and then taken his king to the centre. Instead he played the careless **27.♖c7**
Now Van Foreest grabbed his chance.
27...e5! Preparing a positional exchange sacrifice.
28.fxe5

28...♖axb5!
The point. Black is building a fortress.
29.axb5 ♖xb5 30.♖d8+ ♔h7

31.♖e7 ♗e6 32.♖f8 ♔g6 33.♔f2 ♖b4 34.h3 h5 35.♔g3 ♖a4

Just sitting and waiting; White will be unable to make progress.
36.♖d8 ♖e4 37.♔f3 ♖xe5

38.e4? This blunder immediately allows the draw.
38...♗g4+ 39.hxg4 hxg4+ 40.♔xg4 ♖xe7
Draw.

In the second game, Adhiban won another pawn, which he managed to convert this time. Van Foreest struck back at once.

Adhiban Baskaran
Jorden van Foreest
Hoogeveen 2017 (match-3)

position after 17.♕c4

The situation is not easy for Black. After 17...a5 White has a promising piece sacrifice: 18.♘xe6! ♖xd1+ 19.♘xd1 ♗xe3 20.♘xg7+ ♔f8 21.♘xe3 ♔xg7 22.♘f5+ ♔f8, and now, after 23.♗a2 ♖xa2 24.♕xa2 ♘xe4 25.♖d4, White has a strong attack, and Black will find it surprisingly hard to extricate himself.
17...♖c8 Probably his best bet.
18.♘xe6! Now too. **18...♗xe3 19.♘xg7+ ♔f8 20.♕xb4+ ♔xg7 21.♕xb6**

Giving up the fight for the initiative. He should have inserted 21.e5!, when after 21...♗xf2+ 22.♔h1 ♖hd8 23.exf6+ ♔h8 24.♖f1 he retains his advantage.
21...♗xb6 22.♖b4 ♖c6 23.e5 ♖e8!

Black takes over the initiative.
24.exf6+ ♖xf6 25.♔h1 ♖fe6 26.h4 ♗c7 27.f4 ♗a8 28.♔g1 ♗a5 29.f5 ♖e1+

30.♔f2?

A terrible blunder. It goes without saying that White should have swapped on e1 first, after which Black is only marginally better.
30...♗xb4 31.♖xe1 ♗c5+ 32.♔f1 ♗xg2+
Winning the exchange and the game.

33.♔xg2 ♖xe1 34.f6+ ♔xf6 35.♗xh7 ♗d4 36.♘d5+ ♔g7 37.♗d3 a5 38.b3 ♖g1+ 39.♔f3 ♖h1 40.♔g4 ♗f6 41.♘e3 ♖xh4+ 42.♔f3 ♔f8 43.♗c4 ♗g5 44.♘g4 f5 45.♘e5 ♔g7 46.♔g2 a4 47.bxa4 ♖e4 48.♘f3 ♖xc4 49.♘xg5 ♖g4+ White resigned.

The second match was also decided by a tie-break, Van Foreest winning both games and thereby successfully taking his 'last chance'.

■ ■ ■

Machteld van Foreest

The open tournament was slightly less strong than last year. It was won by the Dutch GM Roeland Pruijssers, but the bulk of the attention went to 10-year-old Machteld van Foreest, the dynasty's youngest scion. Strictly speaking, her rating, at slightly over 1800, was too low for her to be allowed to play in the open group, but the organization had decided to give her a chance nonetheless. She gave an excellent account of herself with 4 out of 9, winning a couple of good games.

Carsten Stanetzek
Machteld van Foreest
Hoogeveen 2017 (5)
Italian Game, Giuoco Pianissimo

1.e4 e5 2.♘f3 ♘c6 3.♗c4 ♗c5
4.0-0 ♘f6 5.d3 h6 6.c3 d6 7.♖e1
♗e6 8.♘bd2 a6 9.♗b3 0-0
10.♘f1 ♗a7 11.h3 ♖e8 12.♗xe6
♖xe6 13.♘g3 d5 14.♕e2 ♕d7

15.♗d2
White is quite passive. The alternatives 15.♗e3 and 15.♘f5 would have been better.
15...♖d8 16.♖ad1 dxe4 17.dxe4
♖d6 Strong tripling.

18.♘f1 ♘h5 19.♖b1 ♕e6 20.b3

20...♕g6
Machteld goes adventuring. With the thematic 20...♖d3 she could have retained a large advantage.
21.♔h2 ♘f6 22.♖bd1 ♕h5
23.♘g3

23...♘g4+
The start of a liquidating combination that will lead to an equal endgame.
24.♔g1 ♗xf2+ 25.♕xf2 ♘xf2
26.♘xh5 ♘xd1 27.♖xd1 ♖d3
28.♔f2 ♖xc3 29.♗xc3 ♖xd1
30.♘xe5
Obvious but wrong. White should first have gone 30.♔e2 to restrict the range of the black rook.

30...♖c1!
An adequate reaction. Now Black will lay claim to the game.
31.♘xc6 ♖xc3 32.♘d8 b6
33.♘f4 ♔f8 34.♘e2 ♖c2 35.♔e3
♔e8
White resigned. ∎

Although she is only 10 years old, Machteld van Foreest is seen by several insiders as the biggest talent of the family.

Maxim Dlugy

CURRENT ELO: 2518

DATE OF BIRTH: January 29, 1966

PLACE OF BIRTH: Moscow, Russia

PLACE OF RESIDENCE: New York, USA

What is your favourite city?
The one I am currently living in.

What was the last great meal you had?
The lobster pasta I made for Anatoly Karpov at my apartment in New York.

What drink brings a smile to your face?
Mai Tai.

Which book would you give to a dear friend?
Grandmaster Insides by Maxim Dlugy – I really put my heart into it.

What book is currently on your bedside table?
Why French Children Don't Talk Back by Catherine Crawford (bringing up a little girl is a nice challenge).

What is your all-time favourite movie?
The Devil's Advocate.

And your favourite TV series?
House.

Do you have a favourite actor?
Al Pacino, Ben Affleck, Anthony Hopkins – the list goes on...

And a favourite actress?
Nicole Kidman.

What music are you currently listening to?
In-Grid, The Beatles.

Is there a painting/work of art that moves you?
I enjoy painting a large, beautiful painting and being surprised how well it comes out. Otherwise, the Impressionists are awesome.

Who is your favourite chess player of all time?
Paul Morphy – sooo far ahead of his peers.

Is there a chess book that had a profound influence on you?
Botvinnik's 3-volume games collection annotated by himself.

What was your best result ever?
World Open 1989 – I scored 8½ from 11 and won clear first, playing nine GMs and two IMs.

And the best game you played?
I beat Wesley So in the last round of the G/10 National Championship three years ago. It felt good!

What was the most exciting chess game you ever saw?
Fedorowicz-Shamkovich in the New York International, played in the early 1980s.

What is your favourite square?
d4 – that's where my pawn goes.

Do chess players have typical shortcomings?
Yes, they are focused too much on their game.

Facebook, Instagram, Snapchat, or?
Facebook and Instagram, although my wife manages the latter.

How many friends do you have on Facebook?
Close to 5000, although most are at best acquaintances.

What is your life motto?
Dum spiro spero – While I breathe, I have hope.

When were you happiest?
Now.

Who or what would you like to be if you weren't yourself?
The sun would be nice.

Which three people would you like to invite for dinner?
Napoleon, Nikola Tesla and Leonardo da Vinci.

What is the best piece of advice you were ever given?
Don't give advice if you're not asked for it.

Is there something you'd love to learn?
How to play the guitar.

Where is your favourite place in the world?
The chessboard.

What is your greatest fear?
Not realizing my ambitions.

And your greatest regret?
The early passing of my grandfather, who was a strong chess player.

How do you relax?
By sleeping tight.

If you could change one thing in the chess world, what would it be?
The FIDE President.

Is a knowledge of chess useful in everyday life?
I truly believe it is.

What is the best thing that was ever said about chess?
Chess makes you smarter!